*Lakeside Cabin*
Season 10, Episode 13

**"Just think like a cloud—
float around the sky
and have a good time."**

Bob Ross®

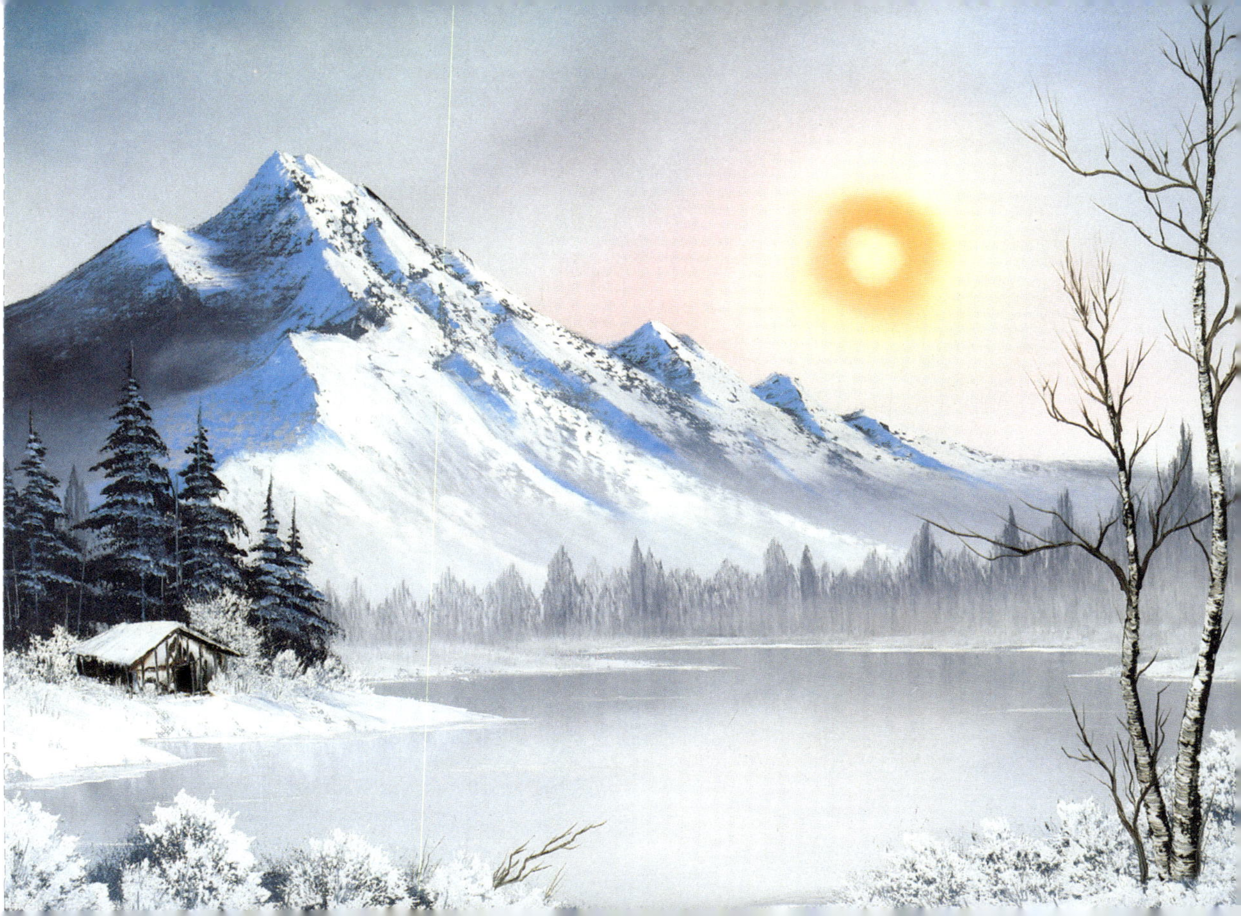

*Winter Frost*
Season 10, Episode 12

**"On this canvas, you're the creator. So you put whatever you want in your world."**

Bob Ross®



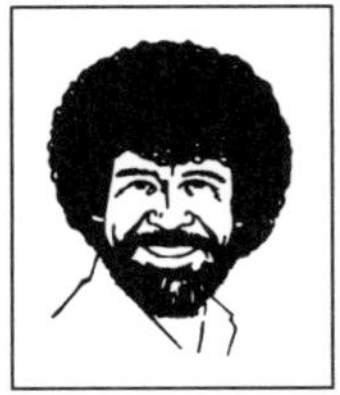

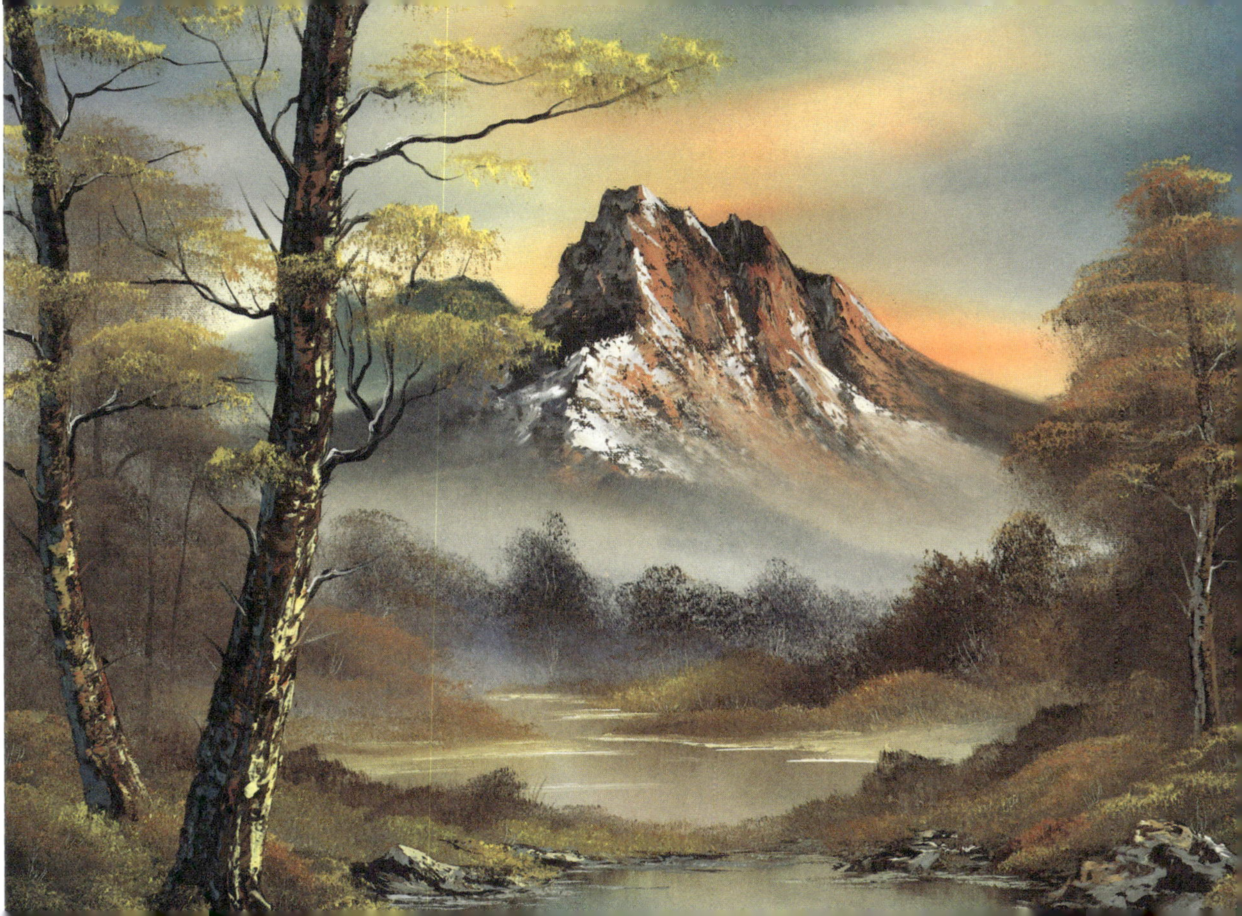

*Mountain Splendor*
Season 7, Episode 8

**“Just let the beautiful little colors play.”**

Bob Ross®

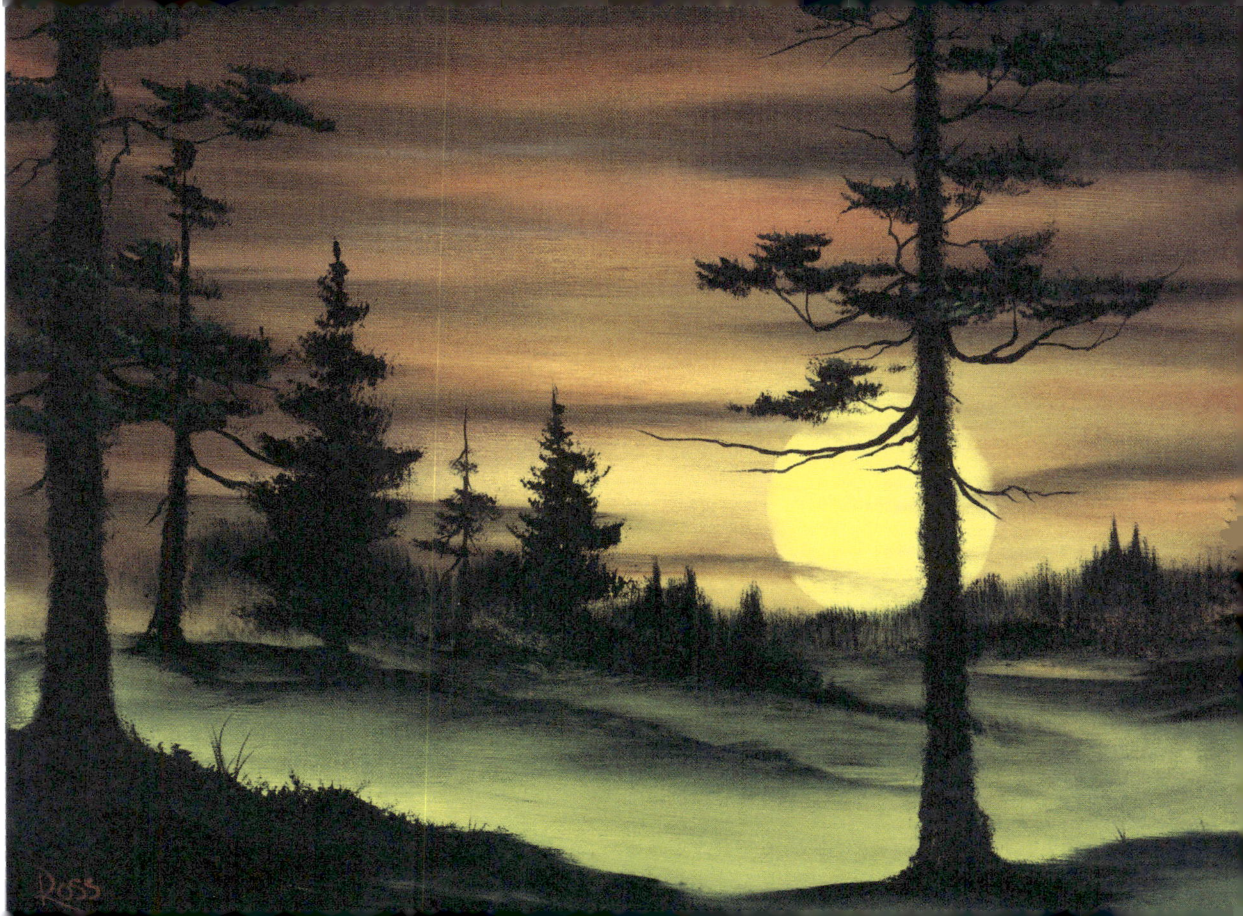
ROSS

*Evergreens at Sunset*
Season 7, Episode 3

**"Let your heart be your guide and take you wherever you want to go."**

Bob Ross®



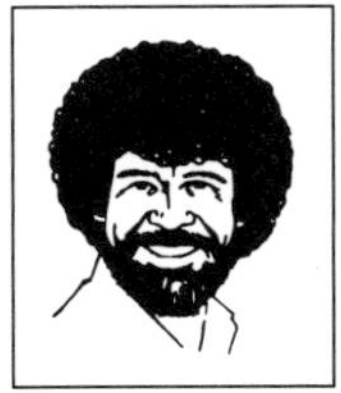

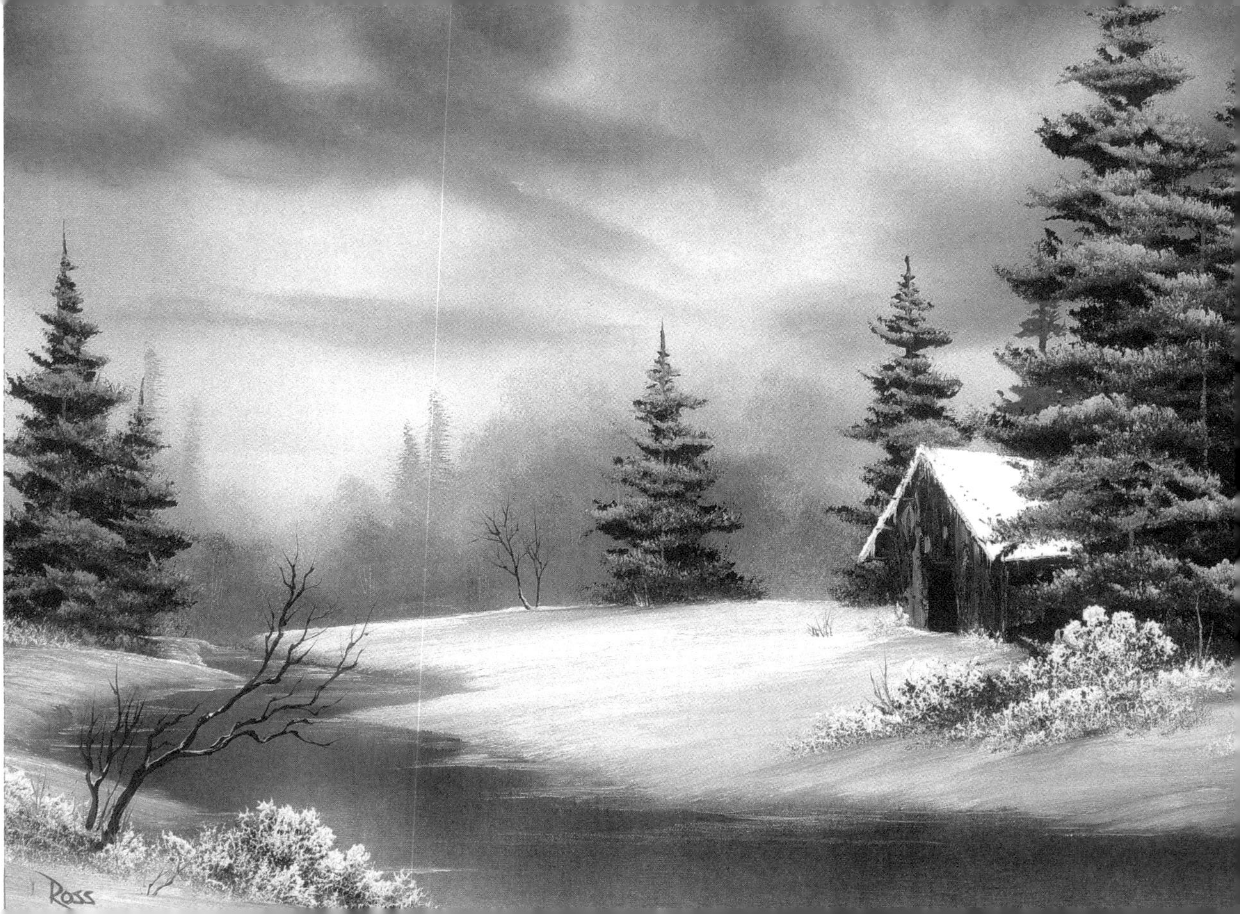
Ross

*Before the Snowfall*
Season 31, Episode 2

**"Bravery test! This is it."**

Bob Ross®

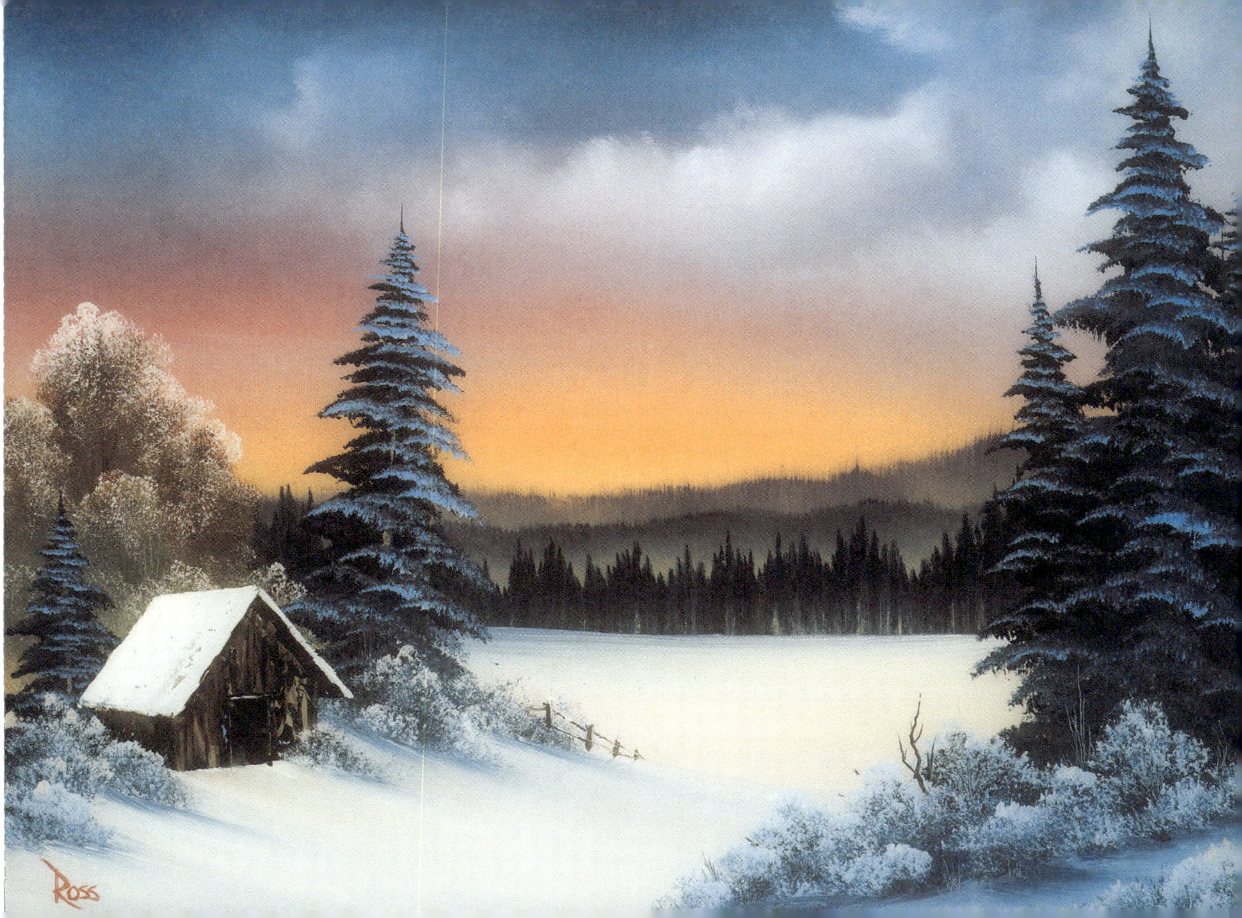
Ross

*Winter's Peace*
Season 30, Episode 3

**"It's a fantastic day here and I hope it is wherever you're at too."**

Bob Ross®


Universe Publishing, A Division of Rizzoli International Publications, Inc., 300 Park Avenue South, New York, NY 10010. www.rizzoliusa.com

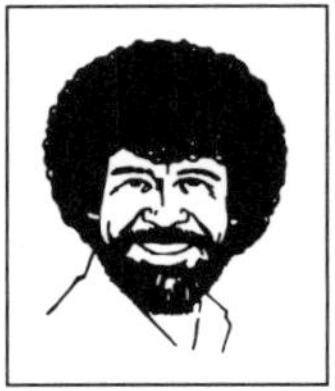

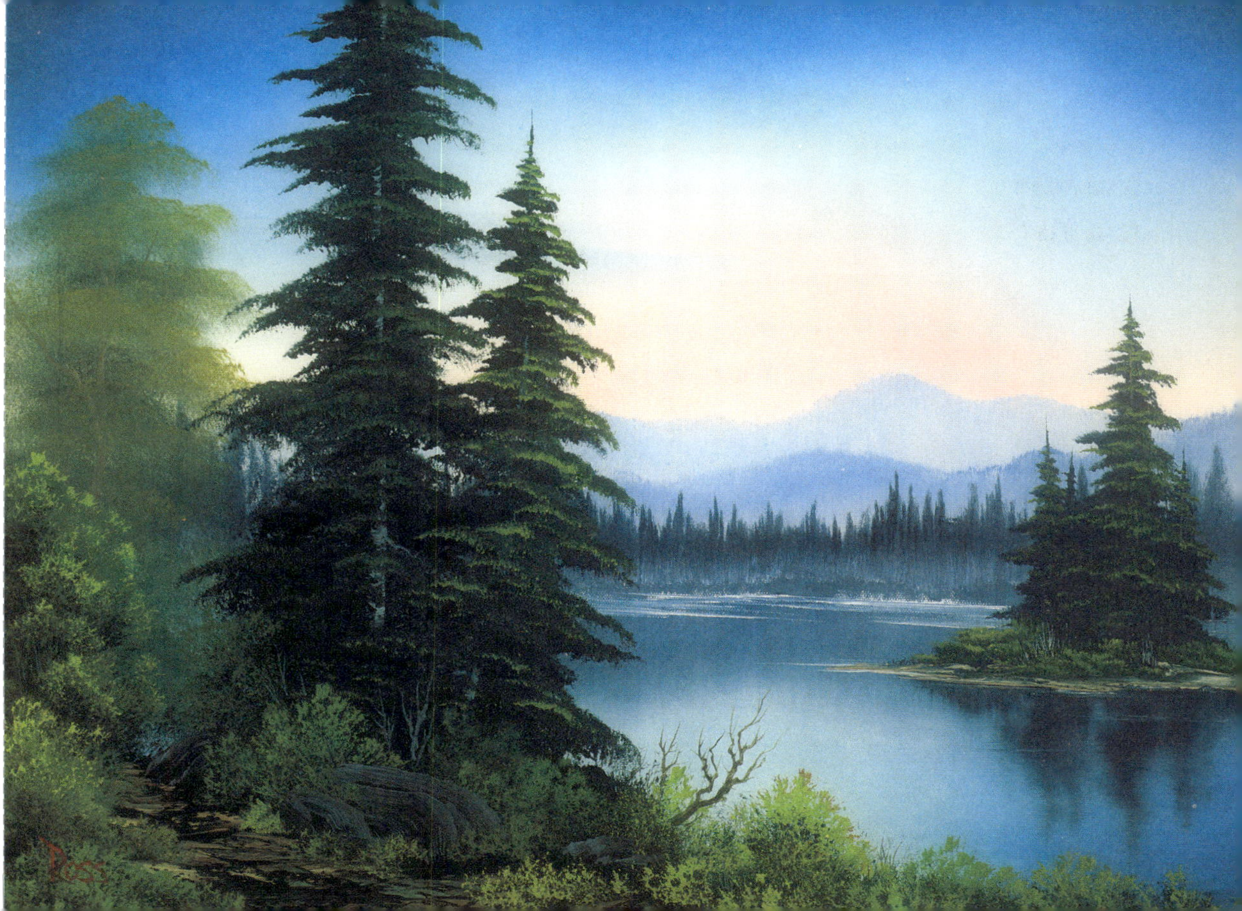

*Island in the Wilderness*
Season 29, Episode 1

**"Anybody can put a little masterpiece on canvas with just a little bit of practice."**

Bob Ross®

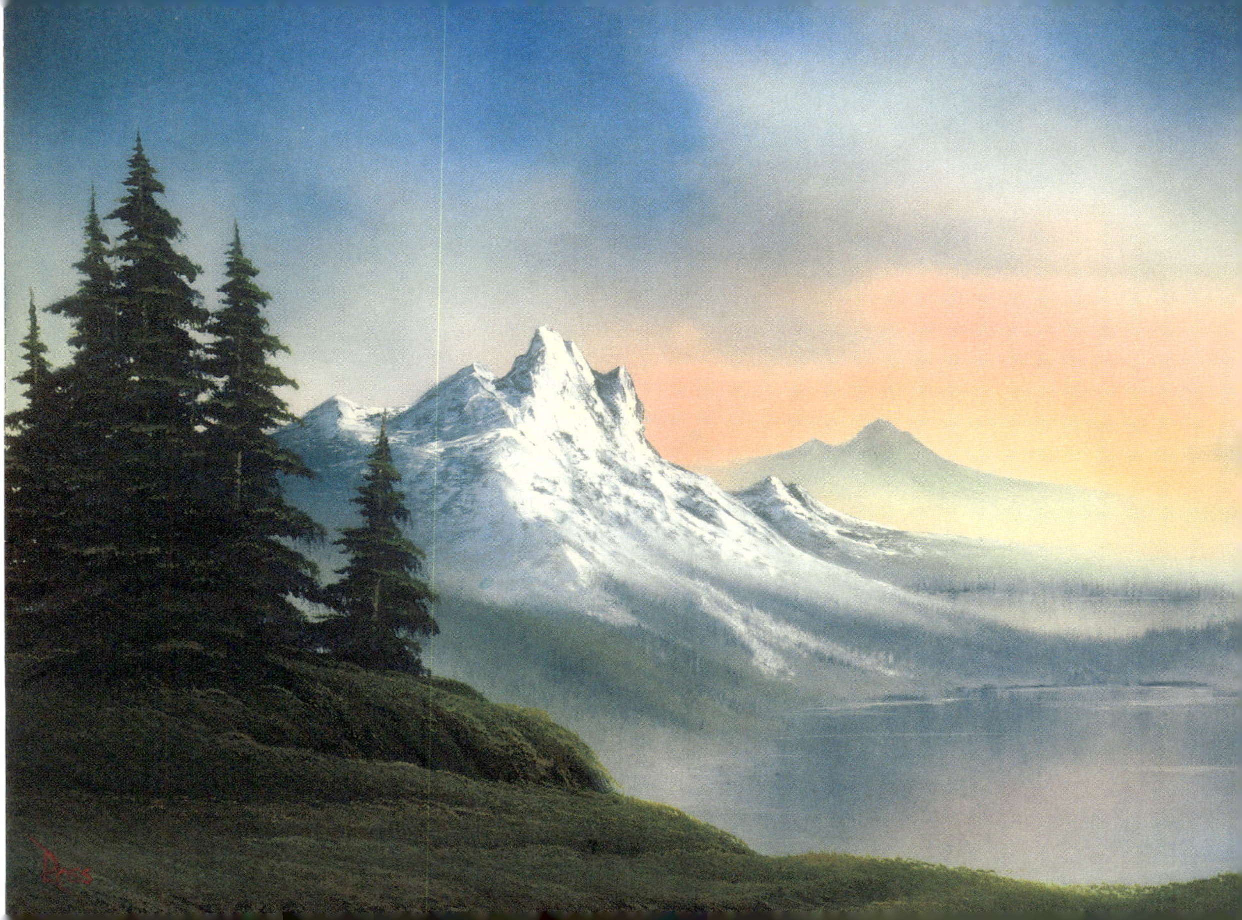

*Under Pastel Skies*
Season 28, Episode 3

**"As you know, we don't make mistakes, we just have happy accidents."**

Bob Ross®



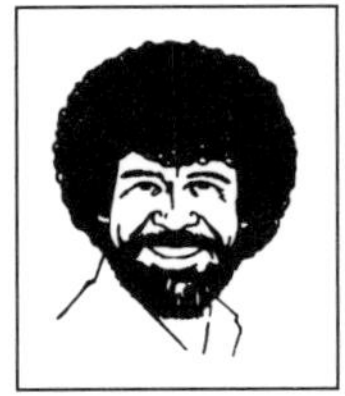

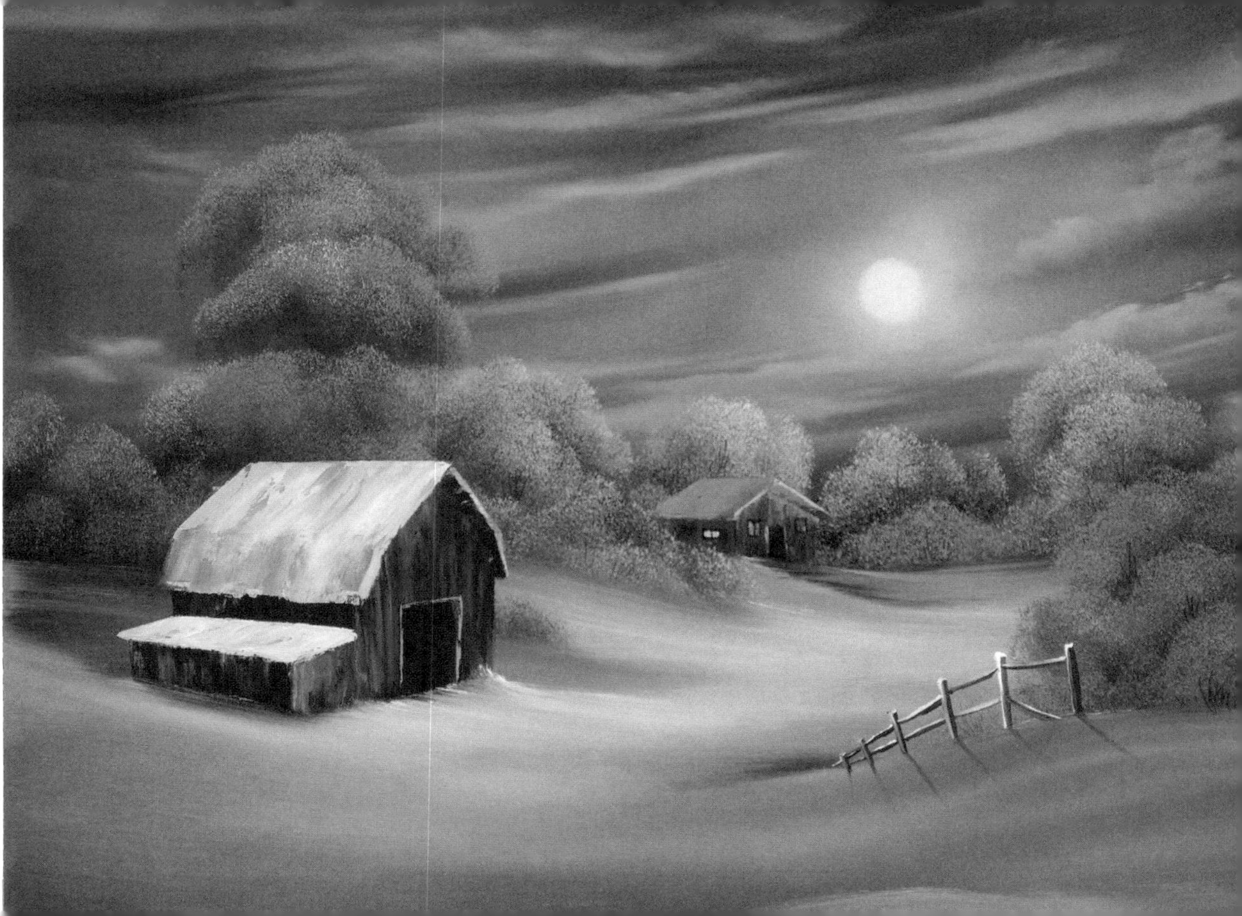

*Evening's Peace*
Season 19, Episode 12

**"What's so fantastic about painting is that it teaches you to see."**

Bob Ross®

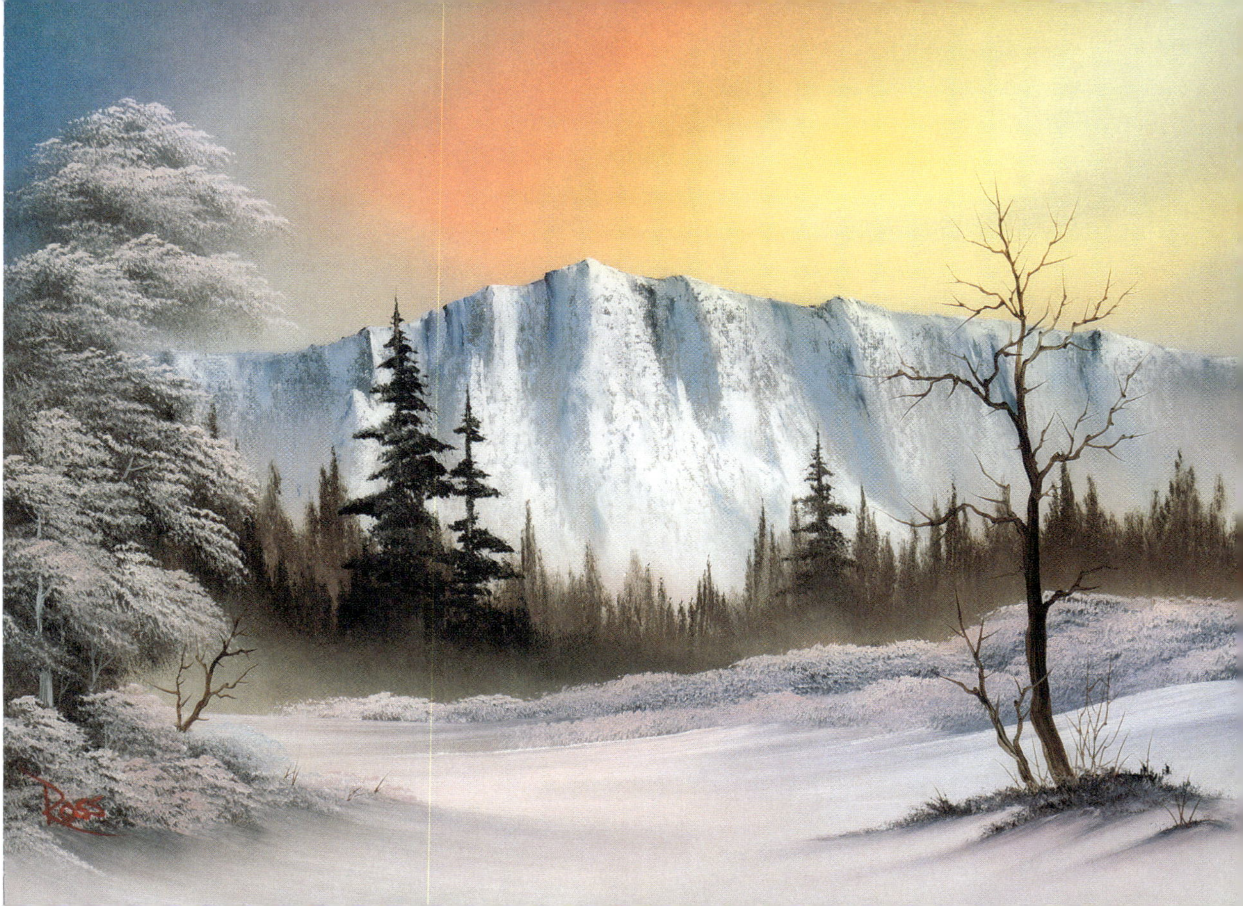
Ross

*Winter in Pastel*
Season 20, Episode 3

**"Just let your imagination take you."**

Bob Ross®



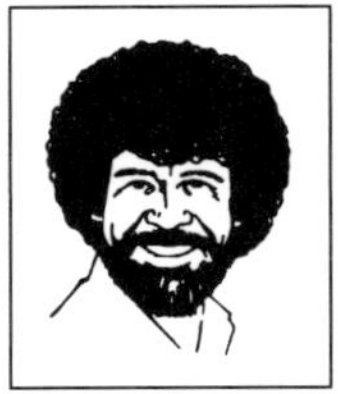

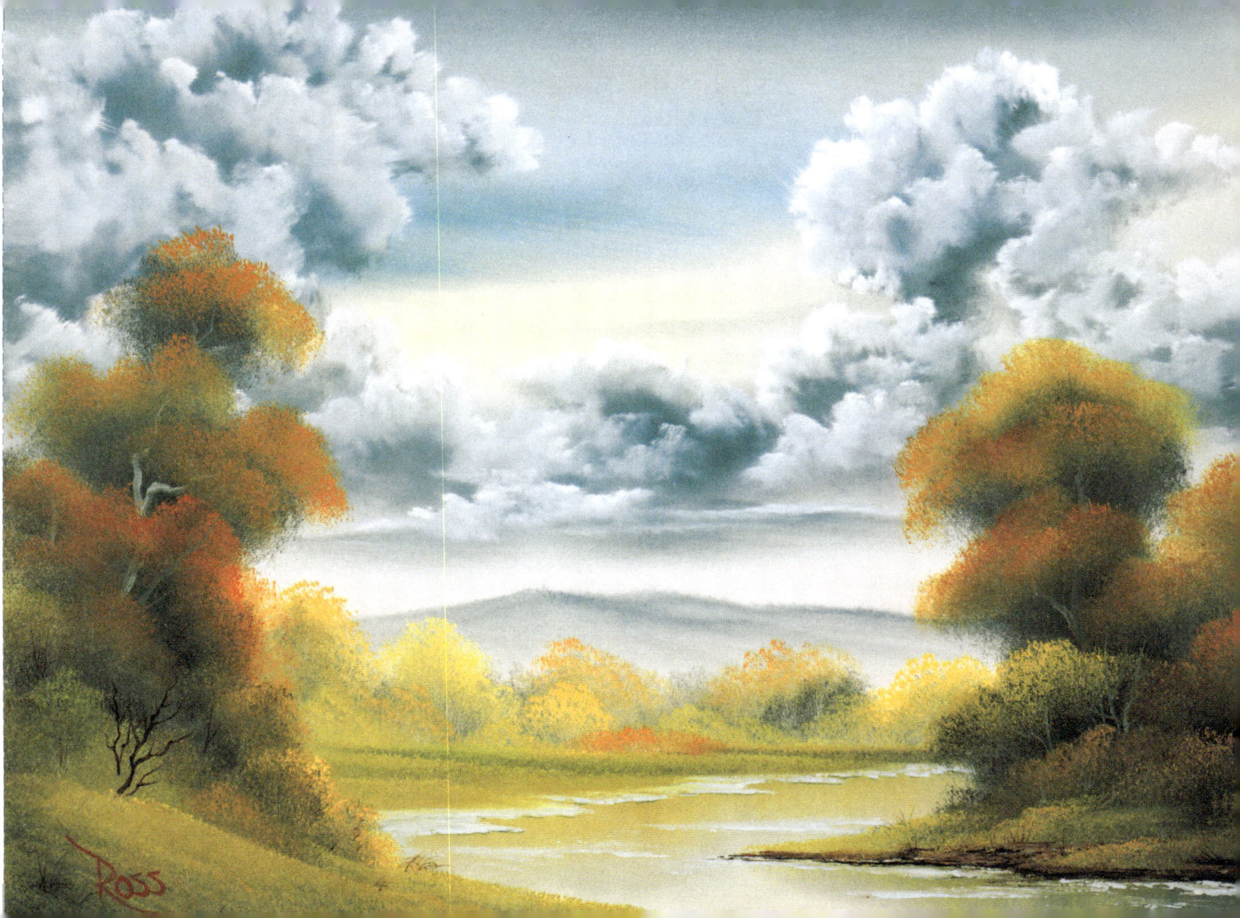
Ross

*Absolutely Autumn*
Season 18, Episode 2

**"You ready to do a fantastic little painting?"**

Bob Ross®

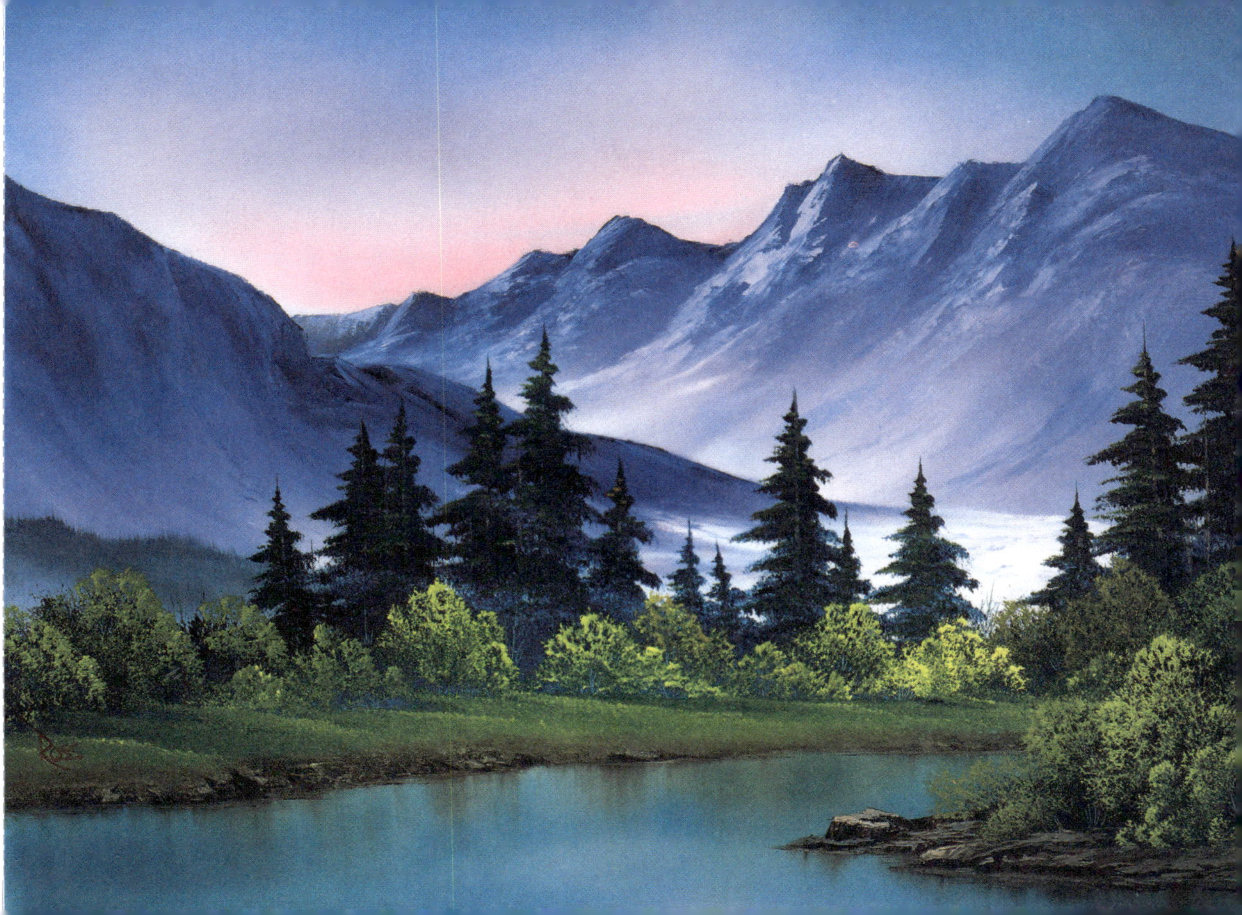

*Camper's Haven*
Season 19, Episode 5

**"Whatever happens that day, let it happen."**

Bob Ross®



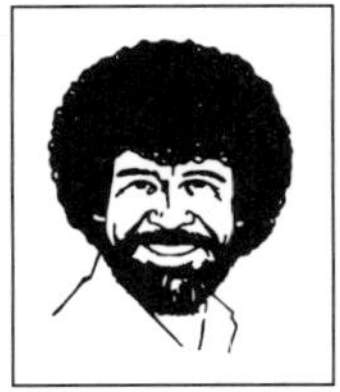

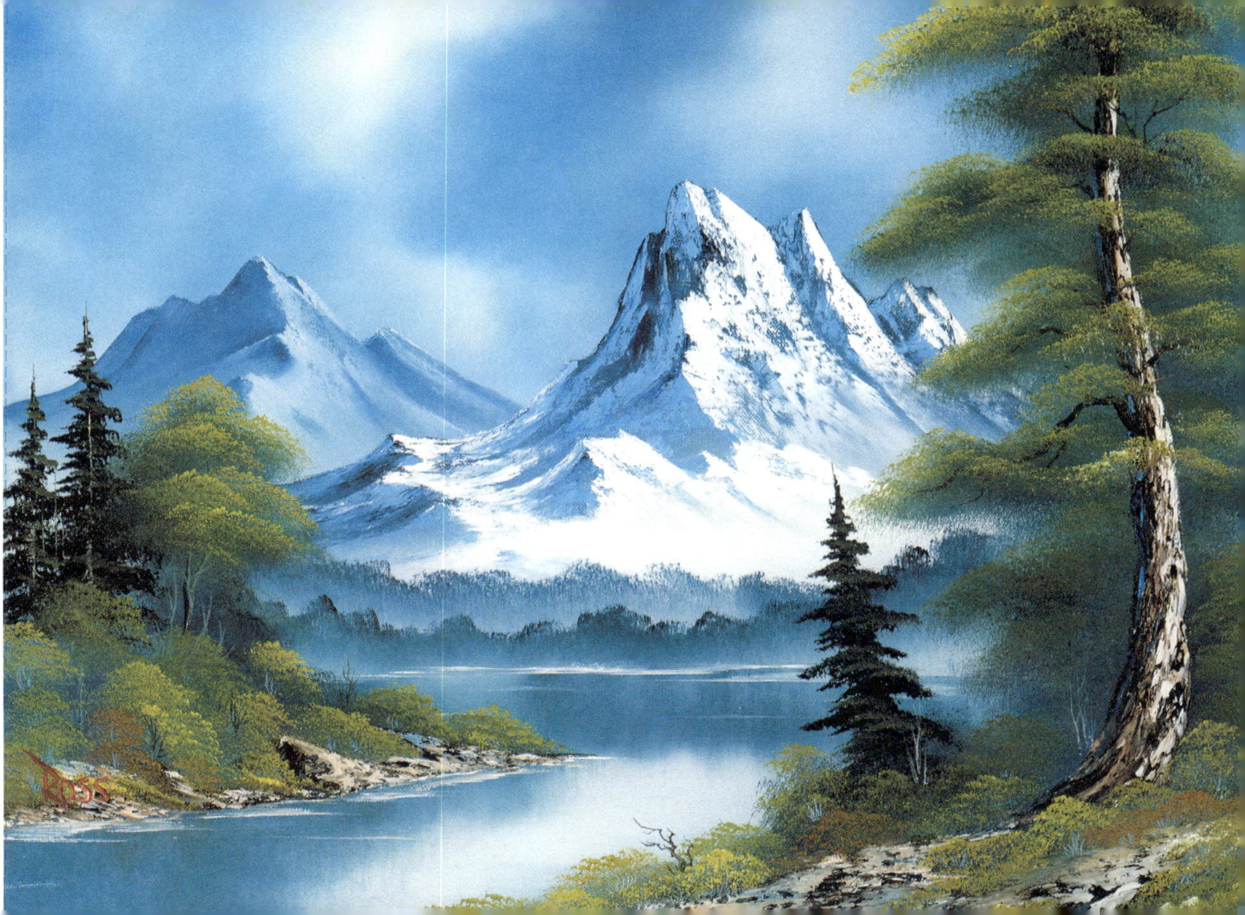
ROSS

*Graceful Mountains*
Season 14, Episode 6

**"Each painting is a learning experience."**

Bob Ross®

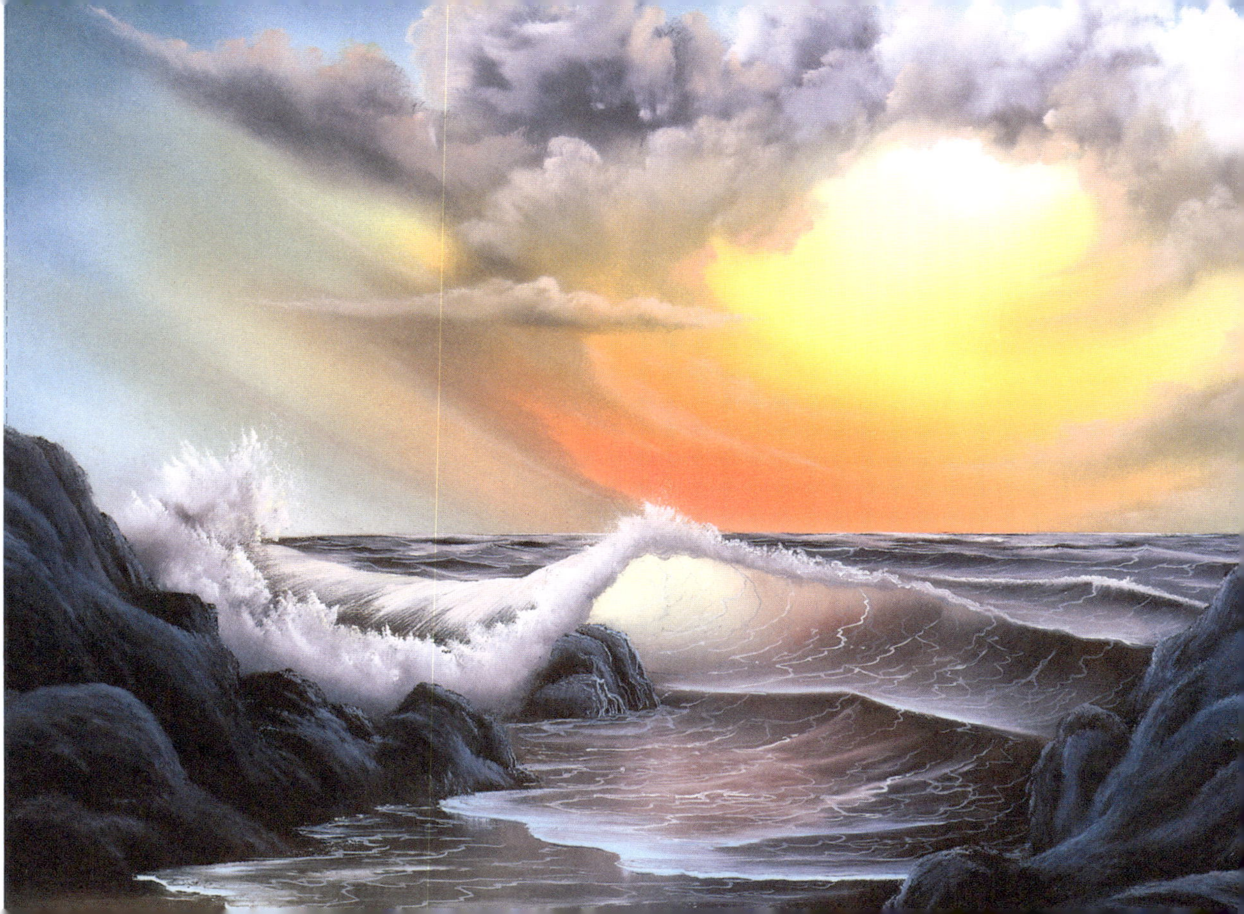

*Stormy Seas*
Season 17, Episode 4

**"Just be brave."**

Bob Ross®



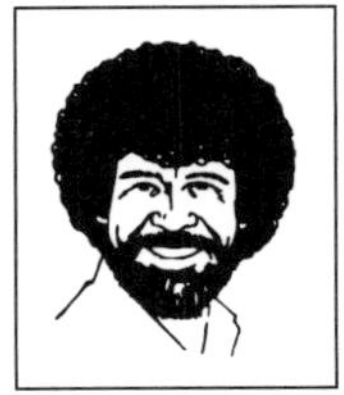

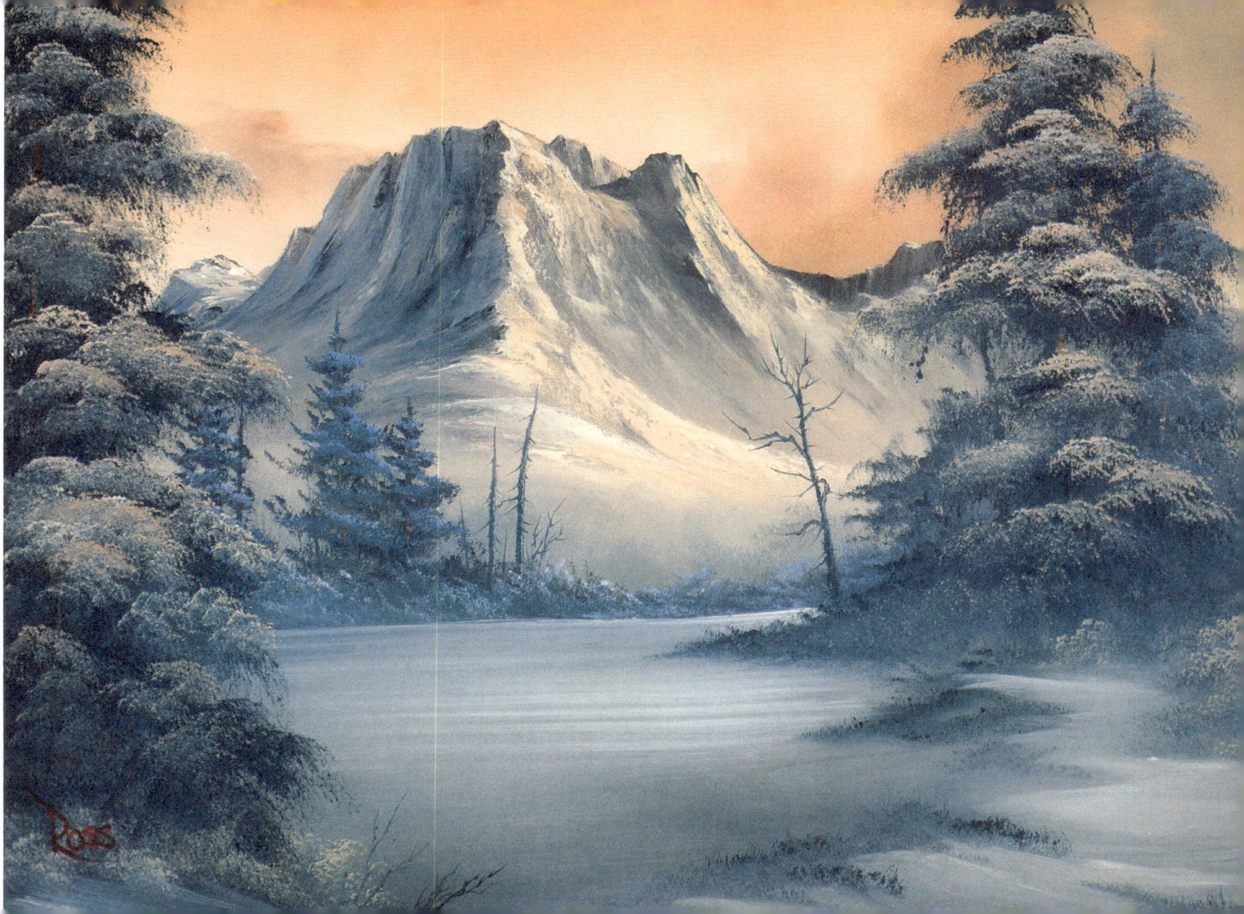

*Mountain Rhapsody*
Season 21, Episode 6

**"Let's get a little crazy—
let's have fun with color."**

Bob Ross®

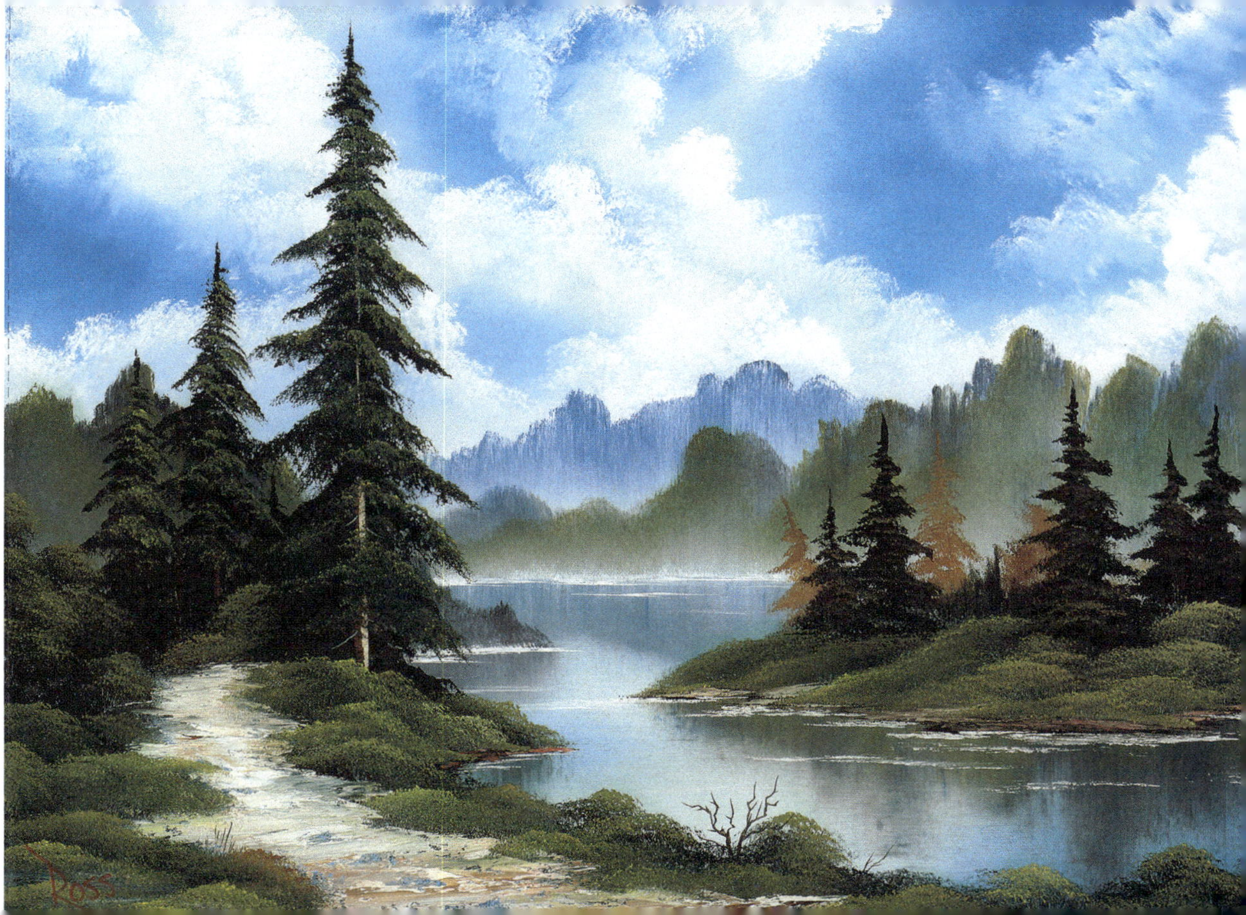
Ross

*Peaceful Haven*
Season 13, Episode 7

**"Just drop in some happy little colors. Let them bounce around and play."**

Bob Ross®


Universe Publishing, A Division of Rizzoli International Publications, Inc., 300 Park Avenue South, New York, NY 10010. www.rizzoliusa.com

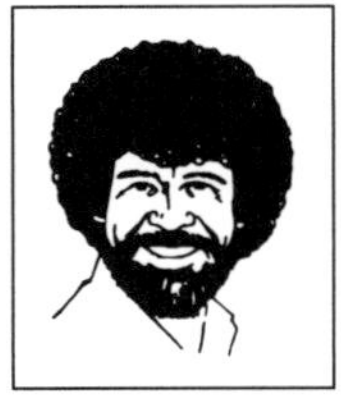

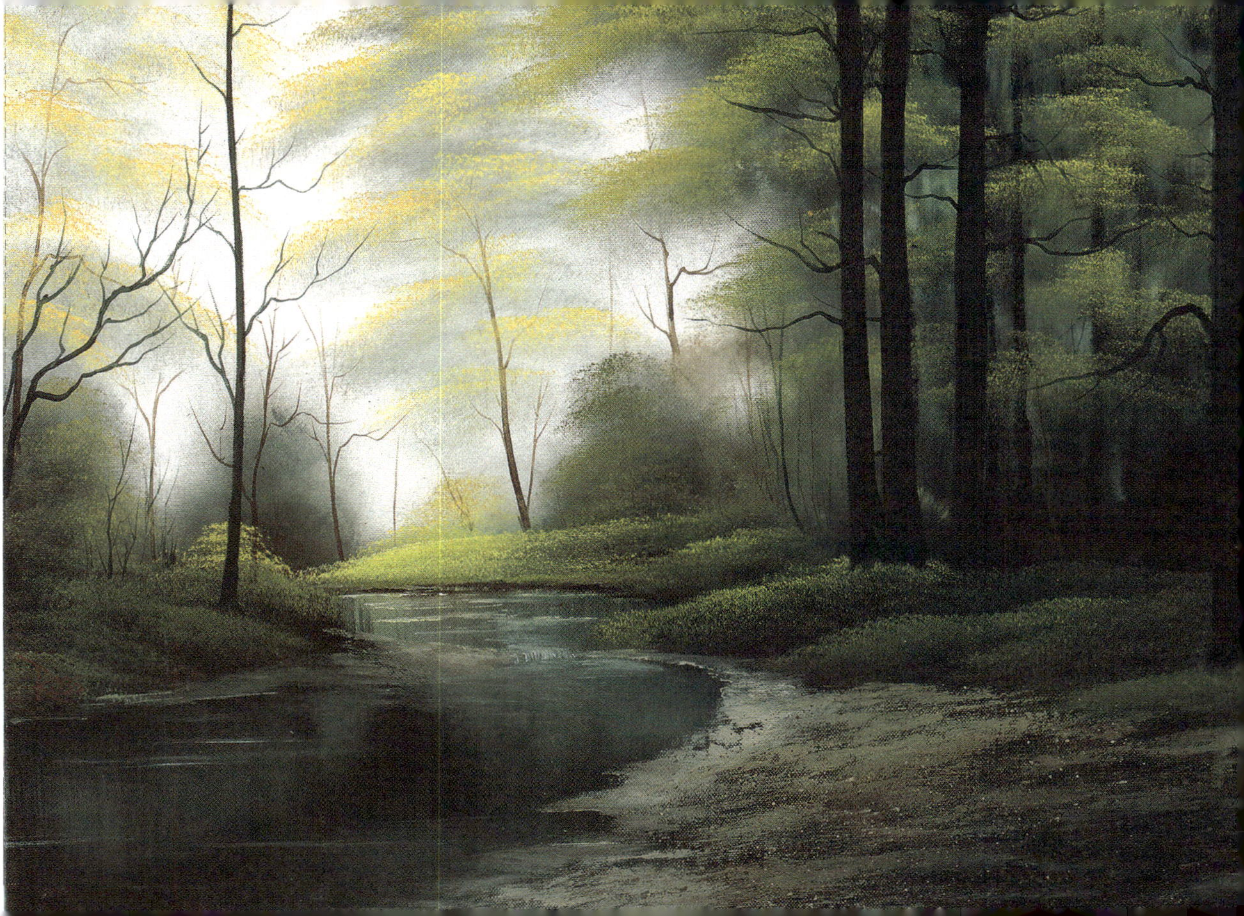

*Hidden Creek*
Season 13, Episode 6

**"A painting will get you started in a world that maybe you haven't tried before. So give it a shot."**

Bob Ross®


Universe Publishing, A Division of Rizzoli International Publications, Inc., 300 Park Avenue South, New York, NY 10010. www.rizzoliusa.com

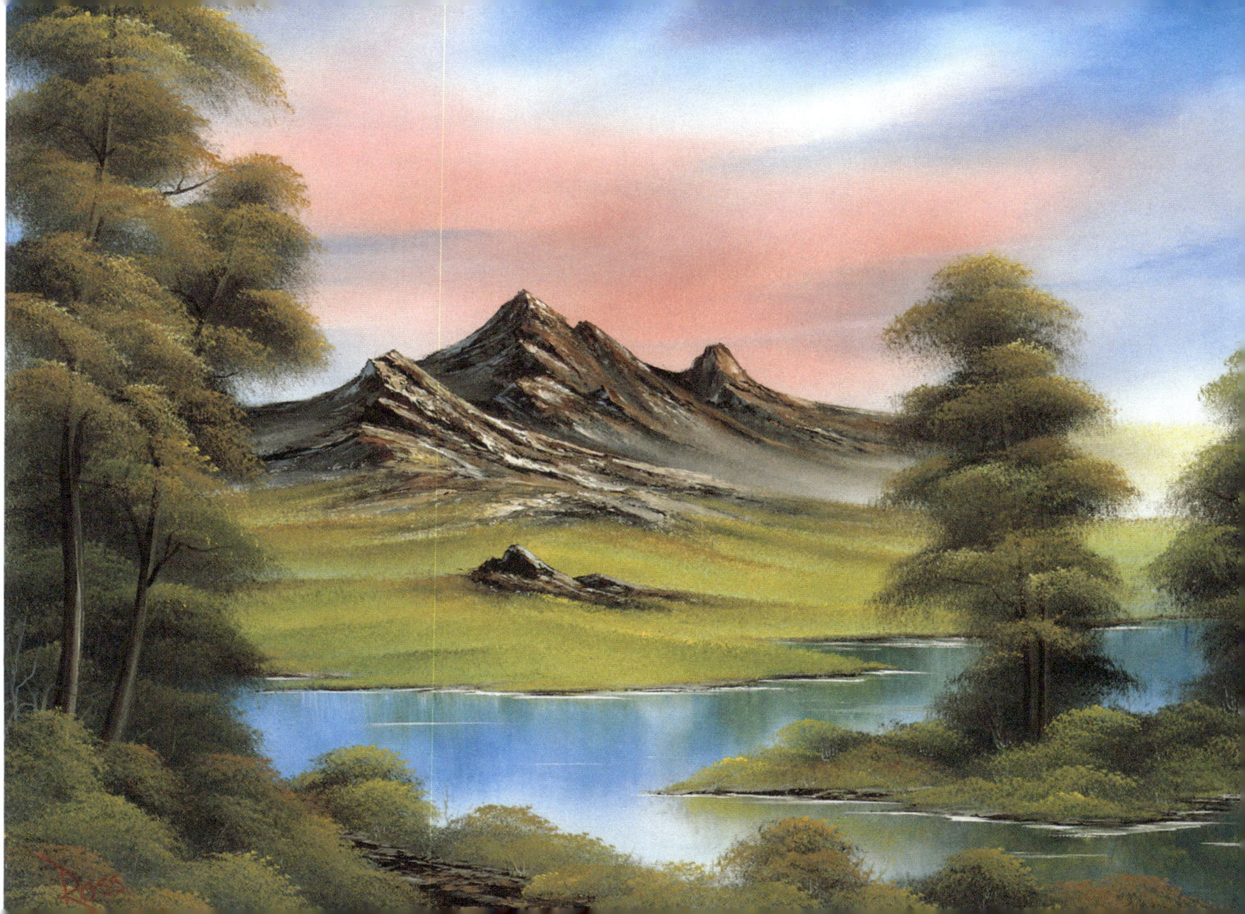
Ross

*Mountain View*
Season 13, Episode 5

**"Just sock some color on
and go from there.
You'll love what happens."**

Bob Ross®


Universe Publishing, A Division of Rizzoli International Publications, Inc., 300 Park Avenue South, New York, NY 10010. www.rizzoliusa.com

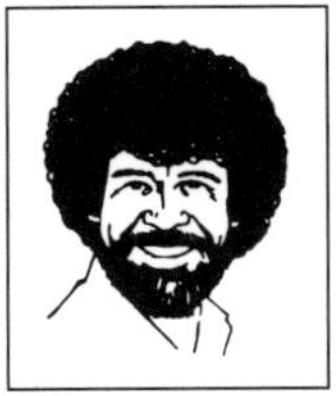

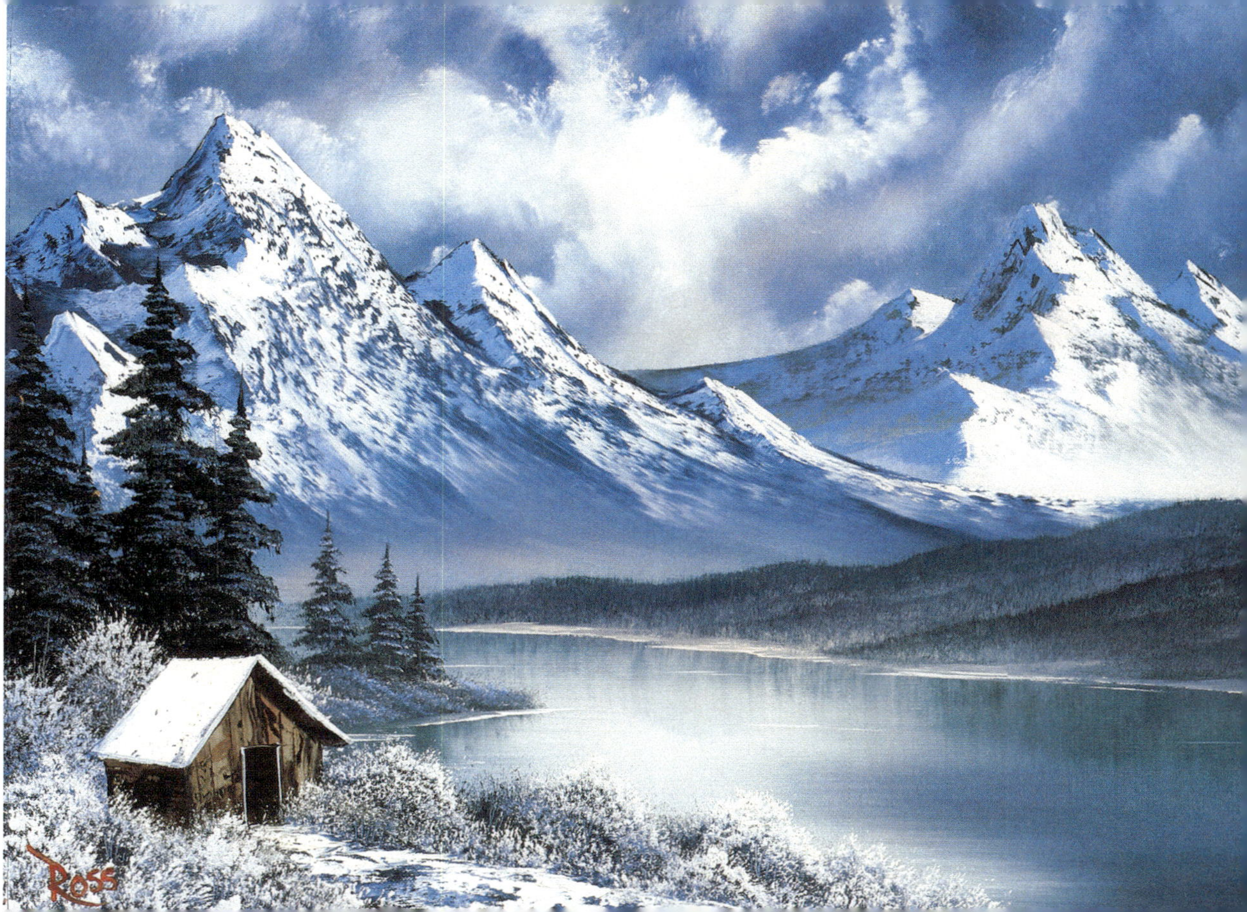
Ross

*Frozen Solitude*
Season 13, Episode 2

**"There's a tremendous amount of pleasure in creating a painting that you see in your mind with your own hands."**

Bob Ross®


Universe Publishing, A Division of Rizzoli International Publications, Inc., 300 Park Avenue South, New York, NY 10010. www.rizzoliusa.com

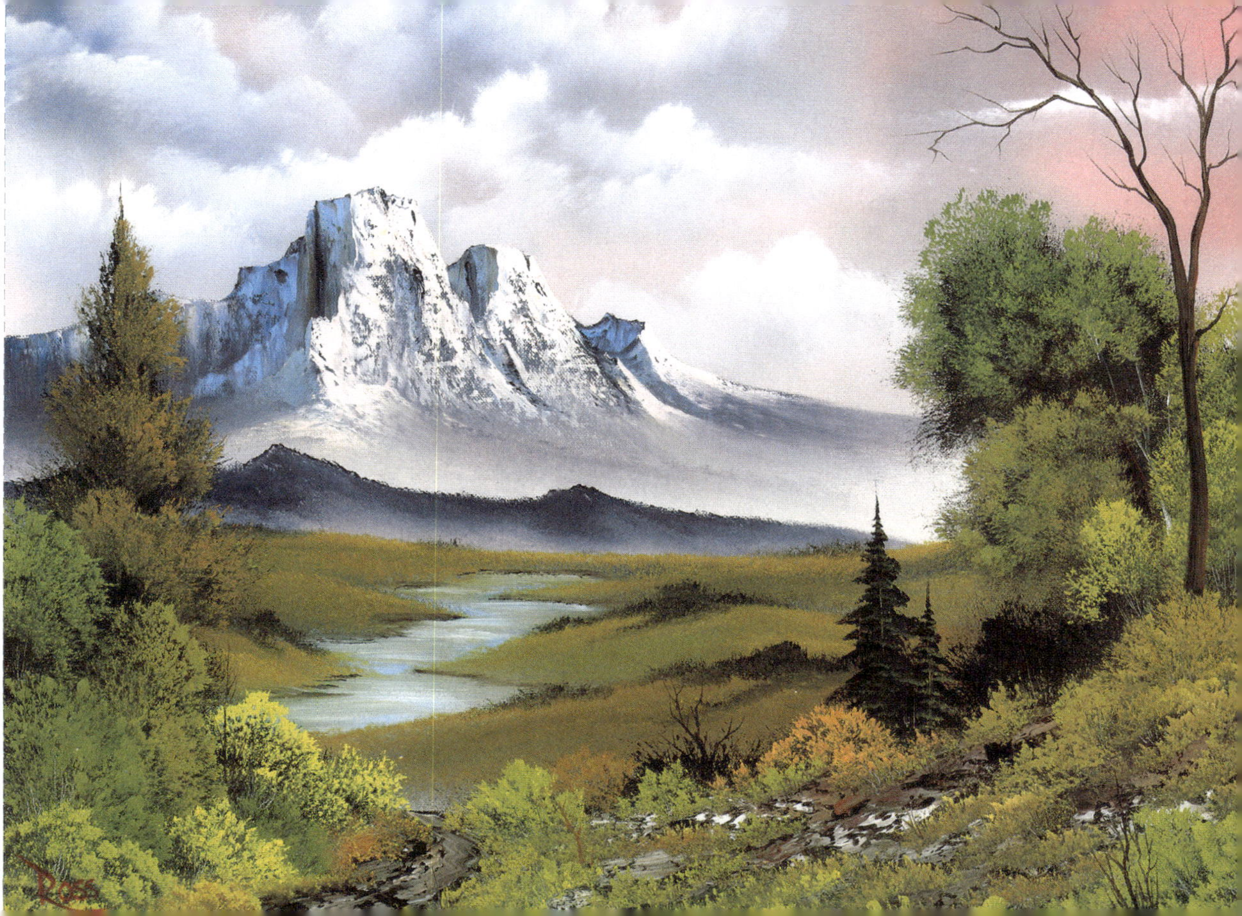
Ross

*Quiet Mountains River*
Season 12, Episode 7

**"We all see nature a little differently, and the way you see it is exactly the way it should be painted."**

Bob Ross®


Universe Publishing. A Division of Rizzoli International Publications, Inc., 300 Park Avenue South, New York, NY 10010. www.rizzoliusa.com

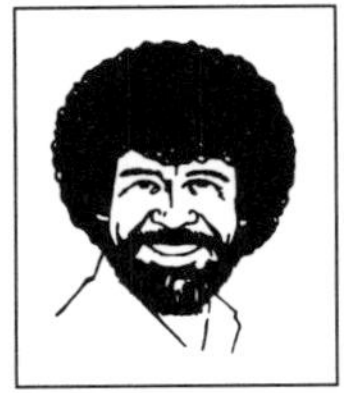

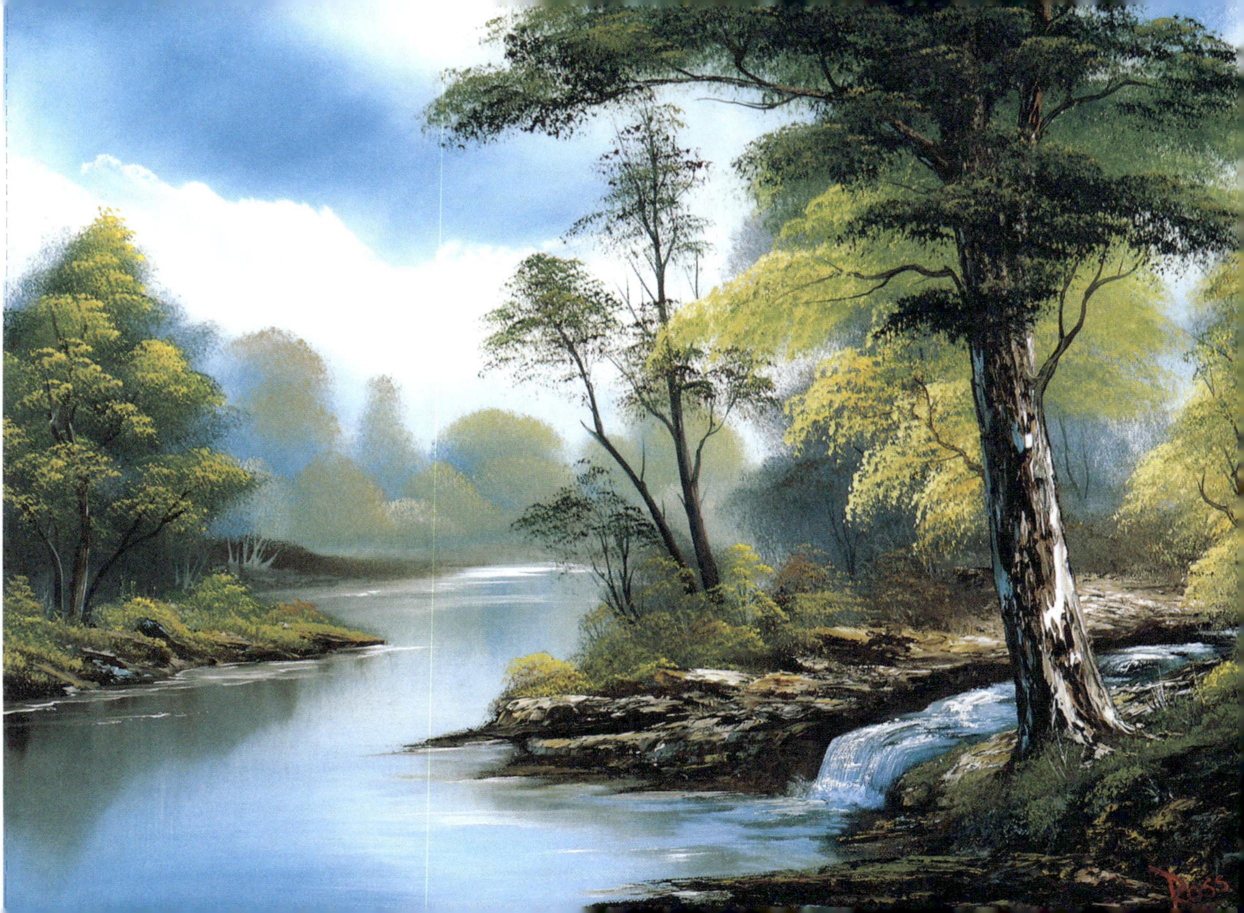
Ross

*Hidden Stream*
Season 11, Episode 4

**"You find what works for you, and that's the way that's right."**

Bob Ross®

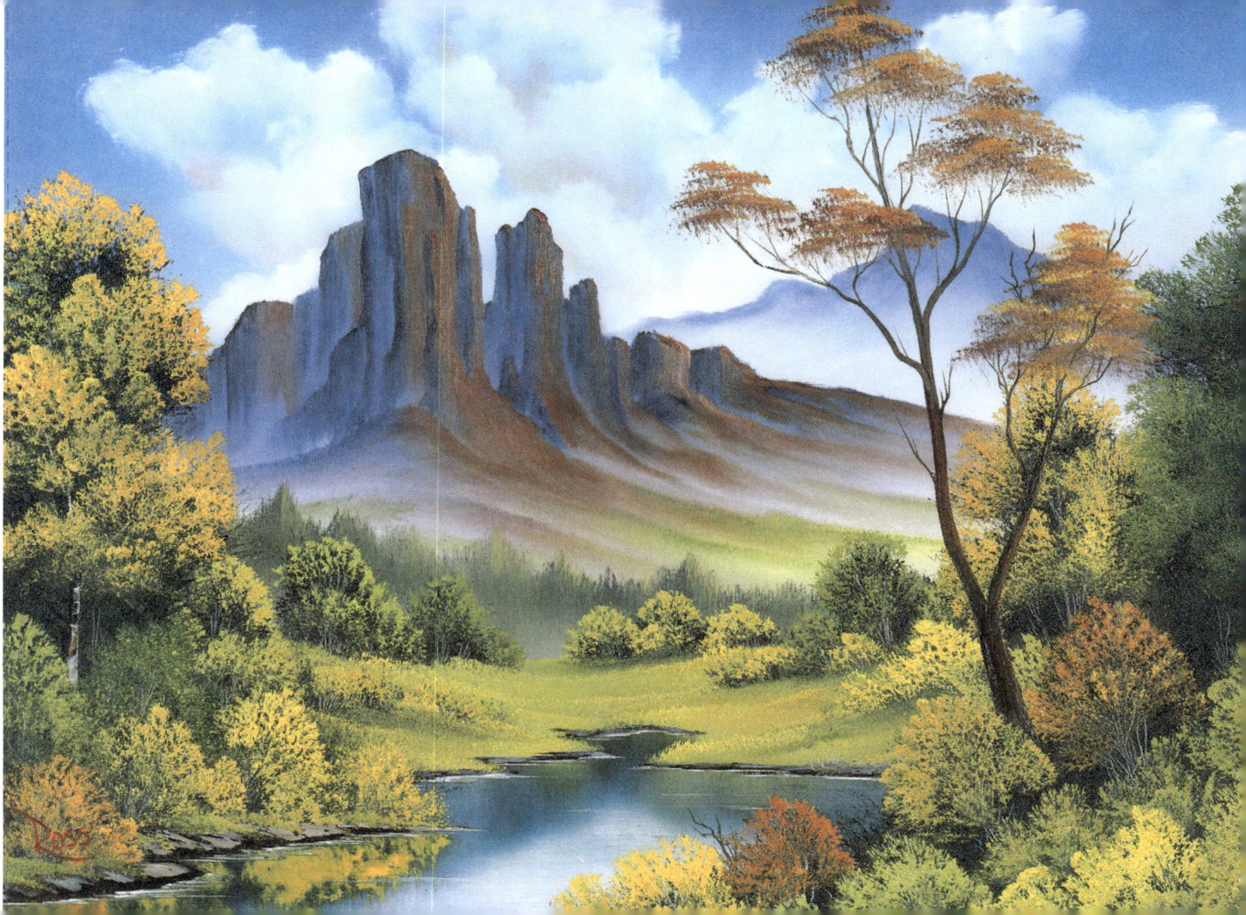
Ross

*Nature's Paradise*
Season 9, Episode 11

**"The first step in being able to do anything is to believe that you can do it."**

Bob Ross®



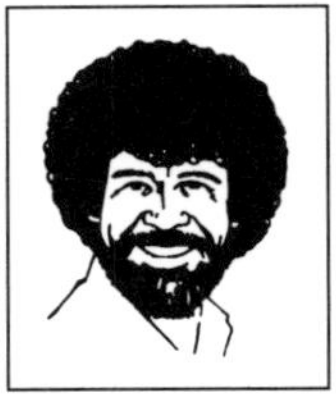

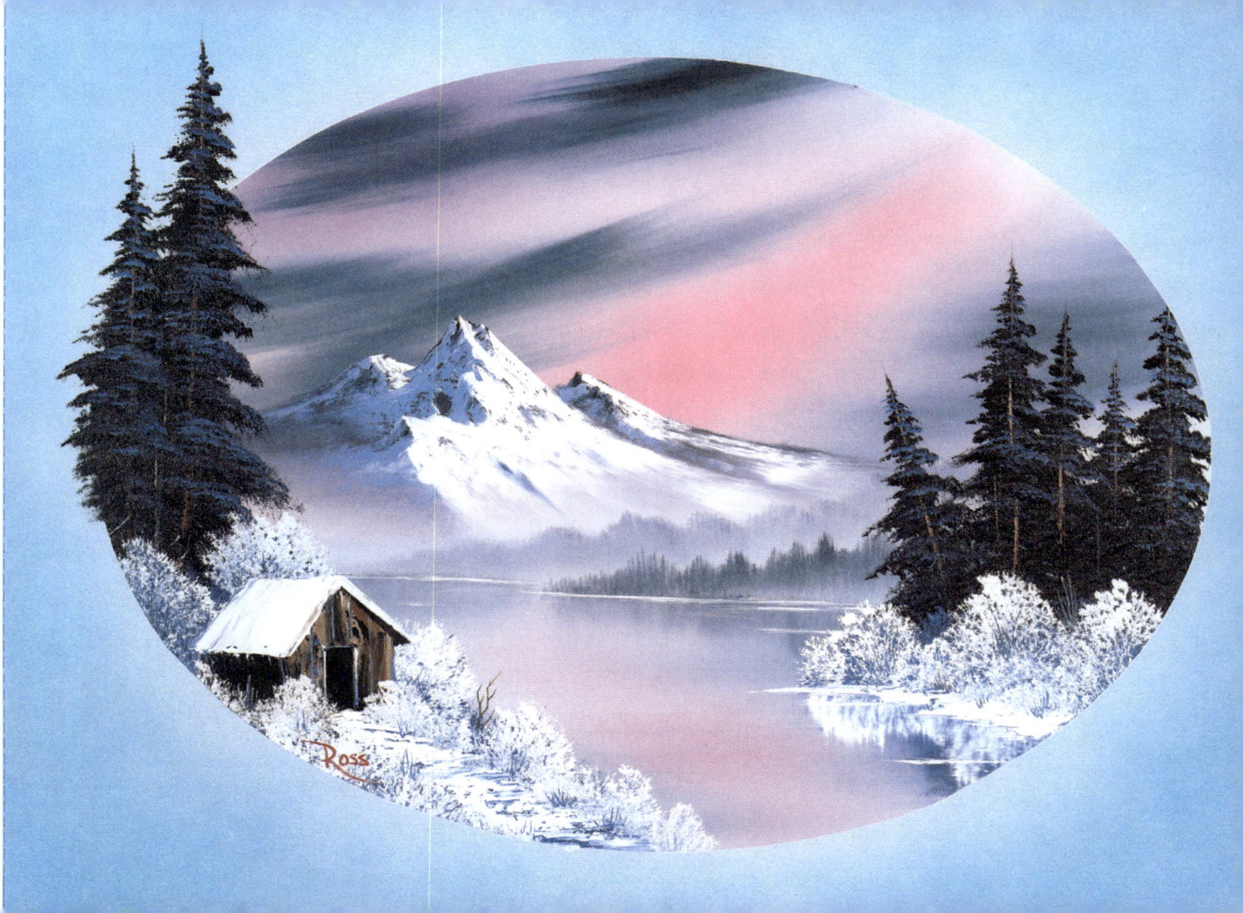
Ross

*Winter Oval*
Season 9, Episode 5

**"You won't believe the things you can make."**

Bob Ross®


Universe Publishing. A Division of Rizzoli International Publications, Inc., 300 Park Avenue South, New York, NY 10010. www.rizzoliusa.com

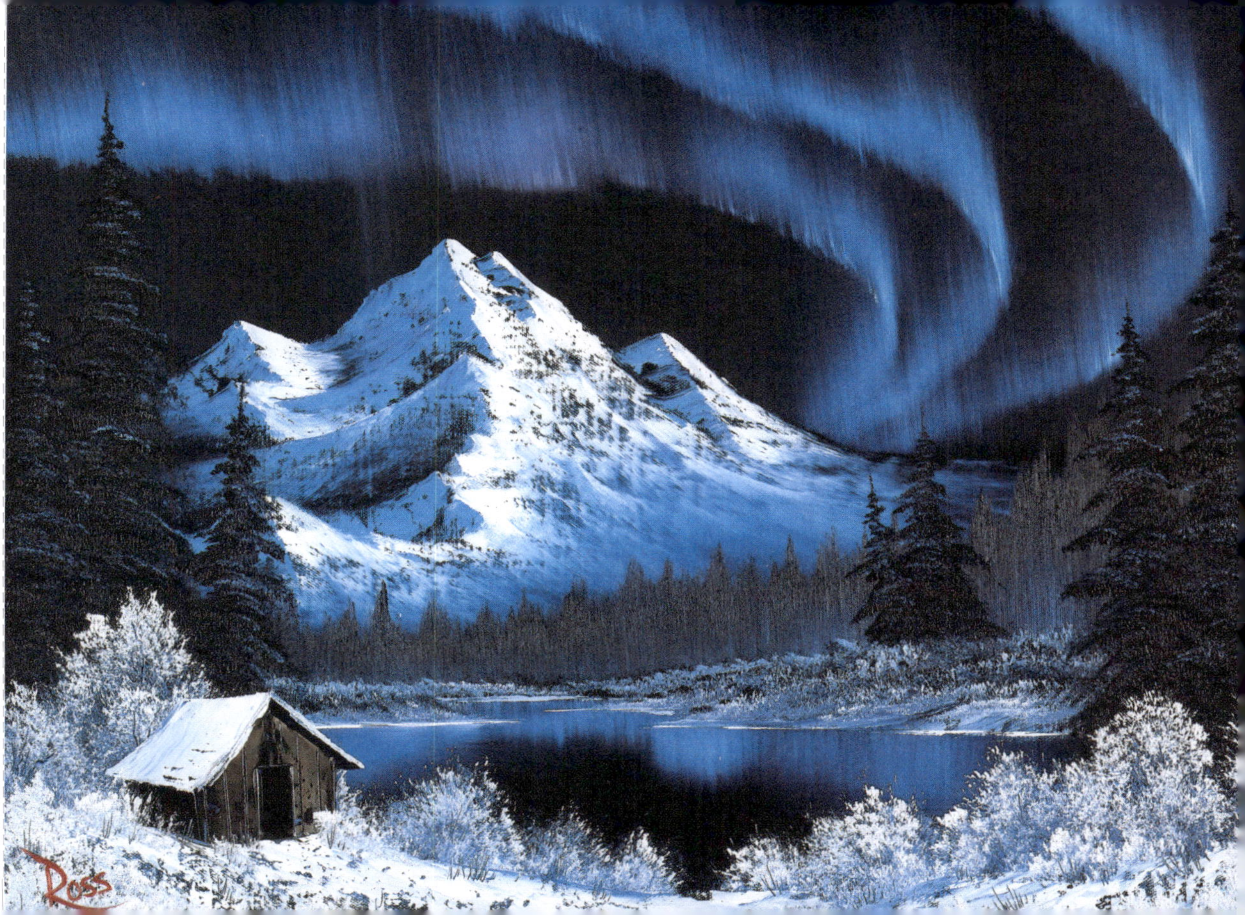
Ross

*Northern Lights*
Season 8, Episode 13

**"Trees and bushes–and everybody–needs a friend."**

Bob Ross®



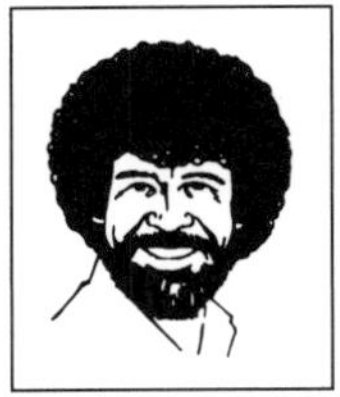

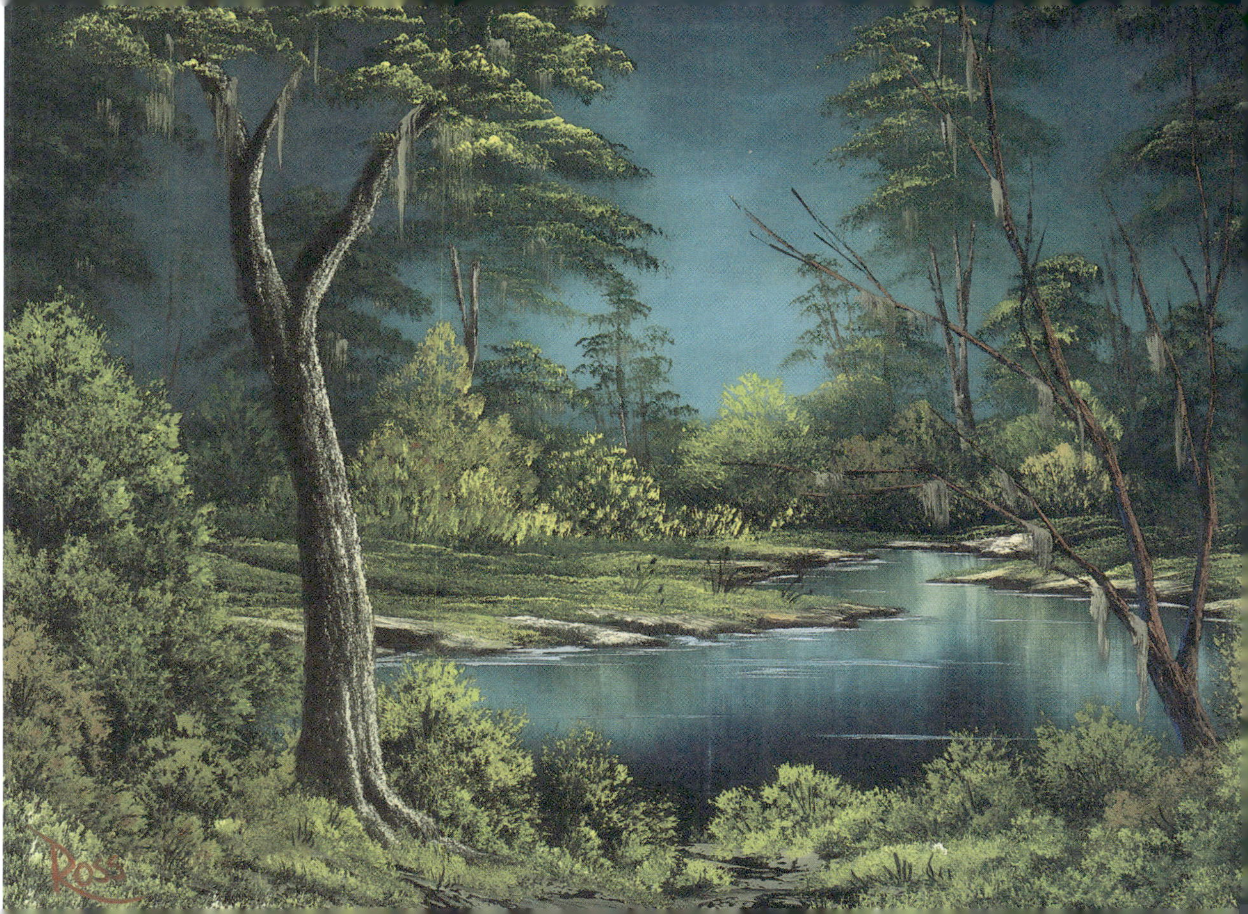
Ross

*Marshlands*
Season 6, Episode 12

**"Make a decision, drop in some color, let it go."**

Bob Ross®

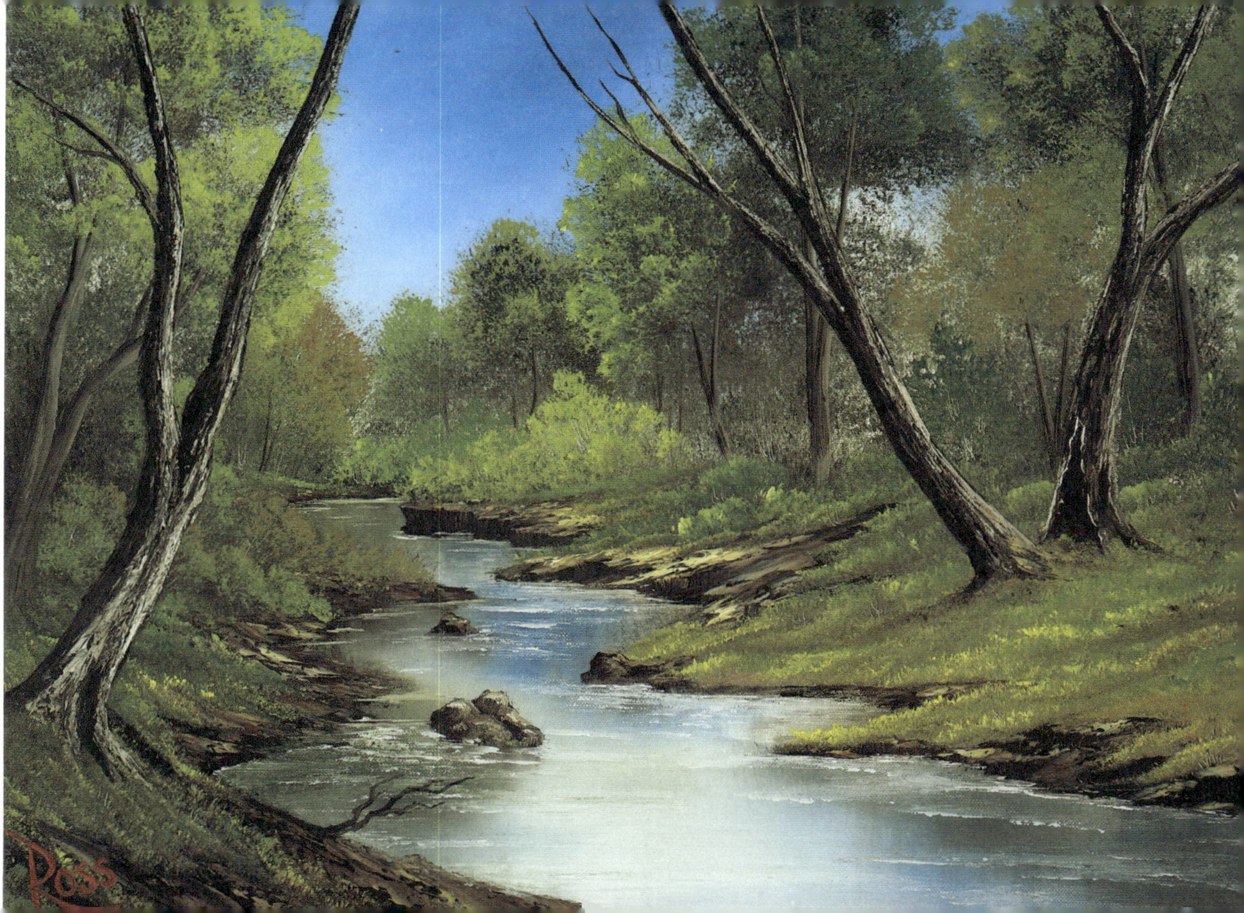
Ross

*Whispering Stream*
Season 6, Episode 4

**"It's your world.
You change things the way
you want them."**

Bob Ross®


Universe Publishing. A Division of Rizzoli International Publications, Inc., 300 Park Avenue South, New York, NY 10010. www.rizzoliusa.com

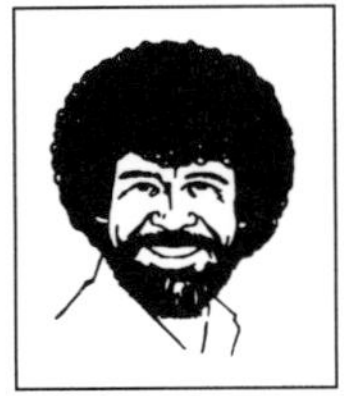

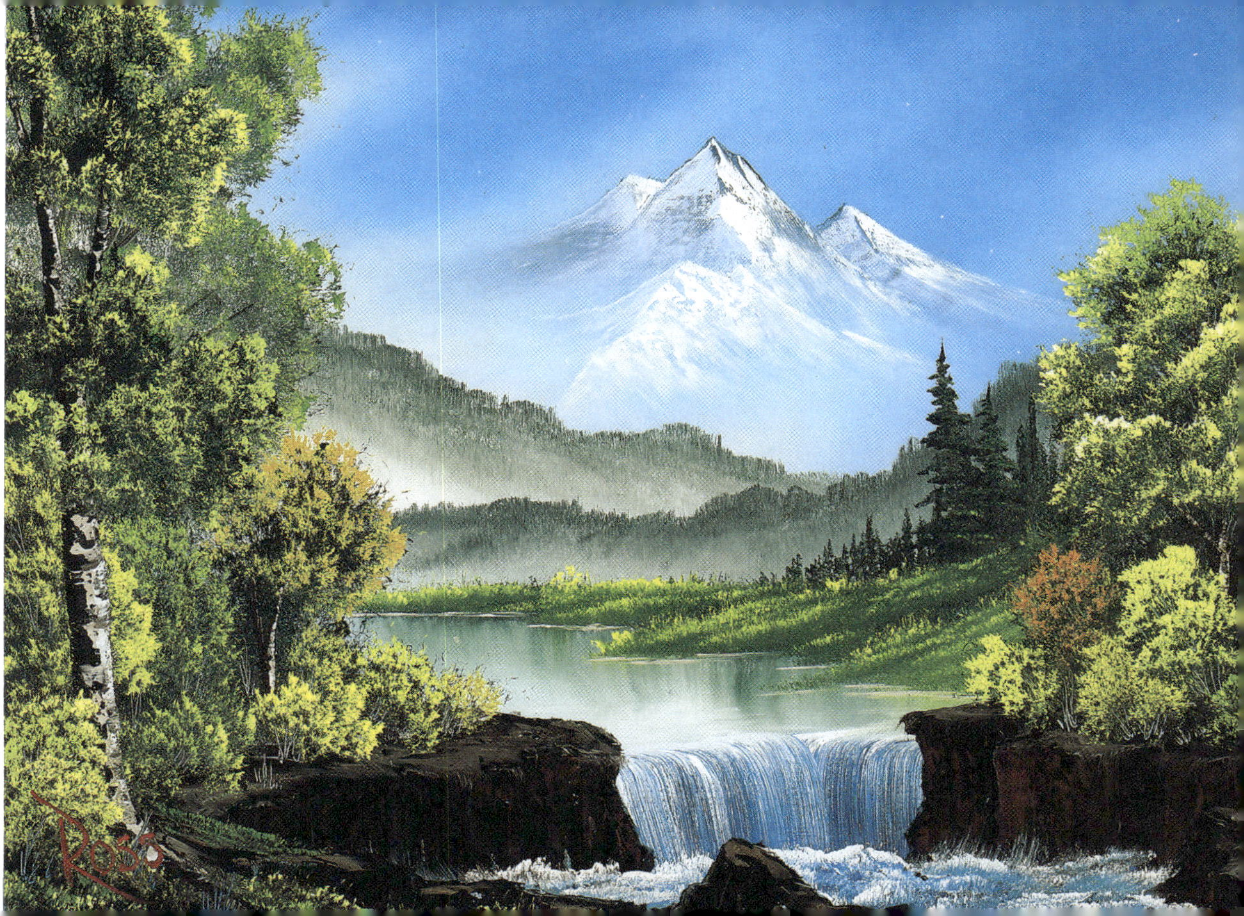
Ross

*Mountain Waterfall*
Season 2, Episode 12

**"We're going to paint a fantastic little picture together."**

Bob Ross®

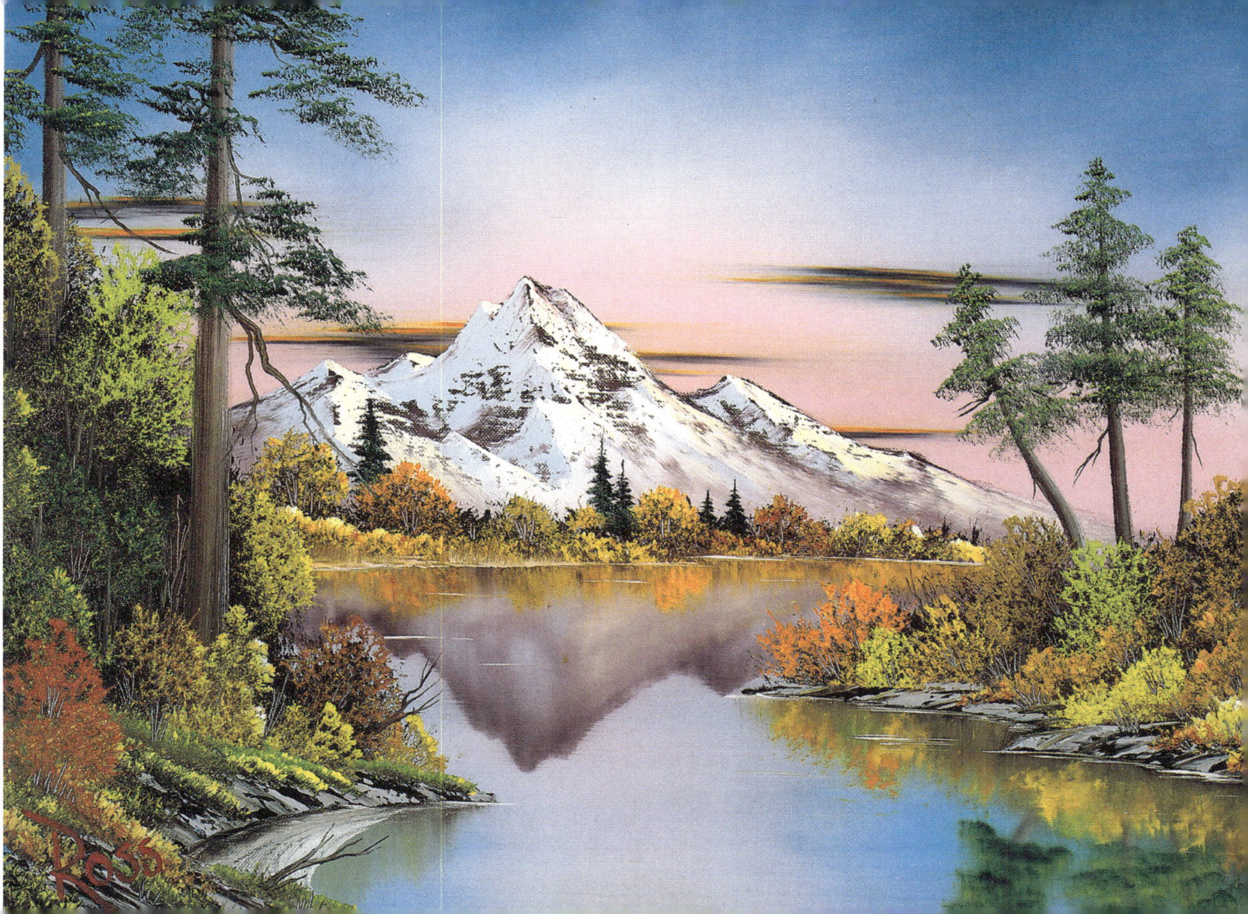
Ross

*Reflections*
Season 2, Episode 8

**"This is your world.
Let it happen."**

Bob Ross®

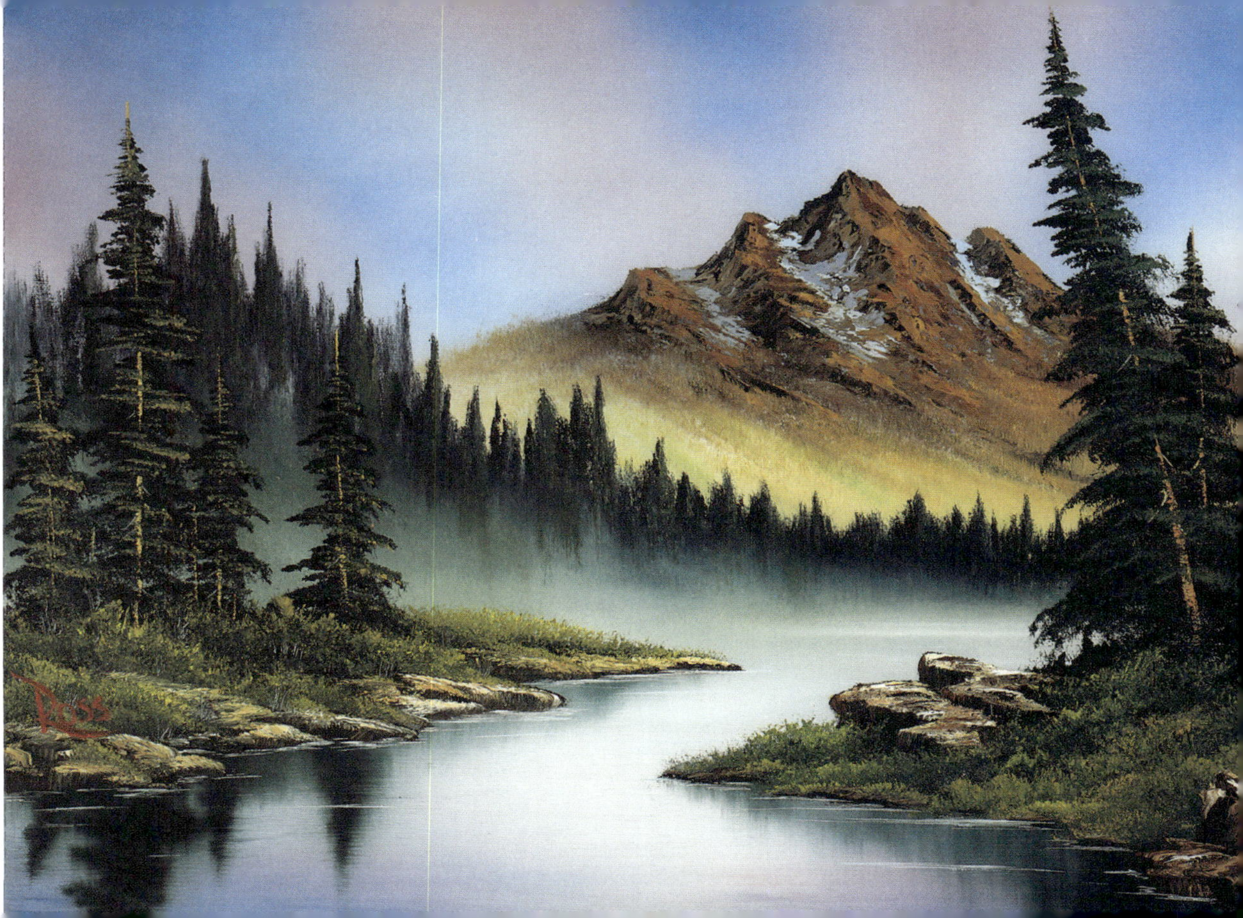

*Morning Mist*
Season 6, Episode 3

**"To me, painting should always be fun. If it's not fun, then change something and make it fun."**

Bob Ross®


Universe Publishing. A Division of Rizzoli International Publications, Inc., 300 Park Avenue South, New York, NY 10010. www.rizzoliusa.com

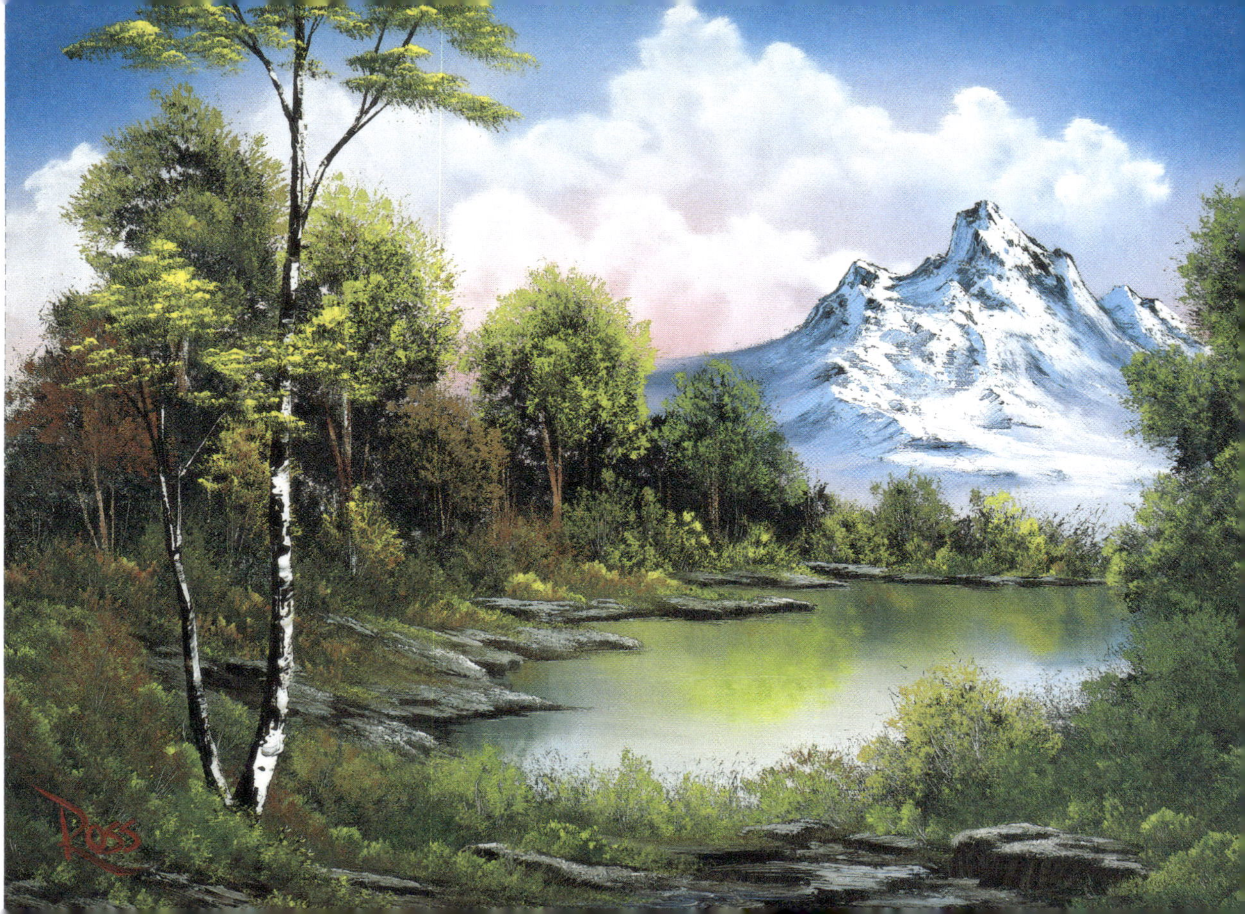
Ross

*Autumn Glory*
Season 5, Episode 11

**"All you have to do is let it out and put it on the canvas. See? It's that easy."**

Bob Ross®


Universe Publishing. A Division of Rizzoli International Publications, Inc., 300 Park Avenue South, New York, NY 10010. www.rizzoliusa.com

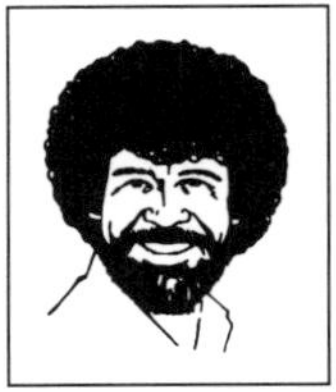

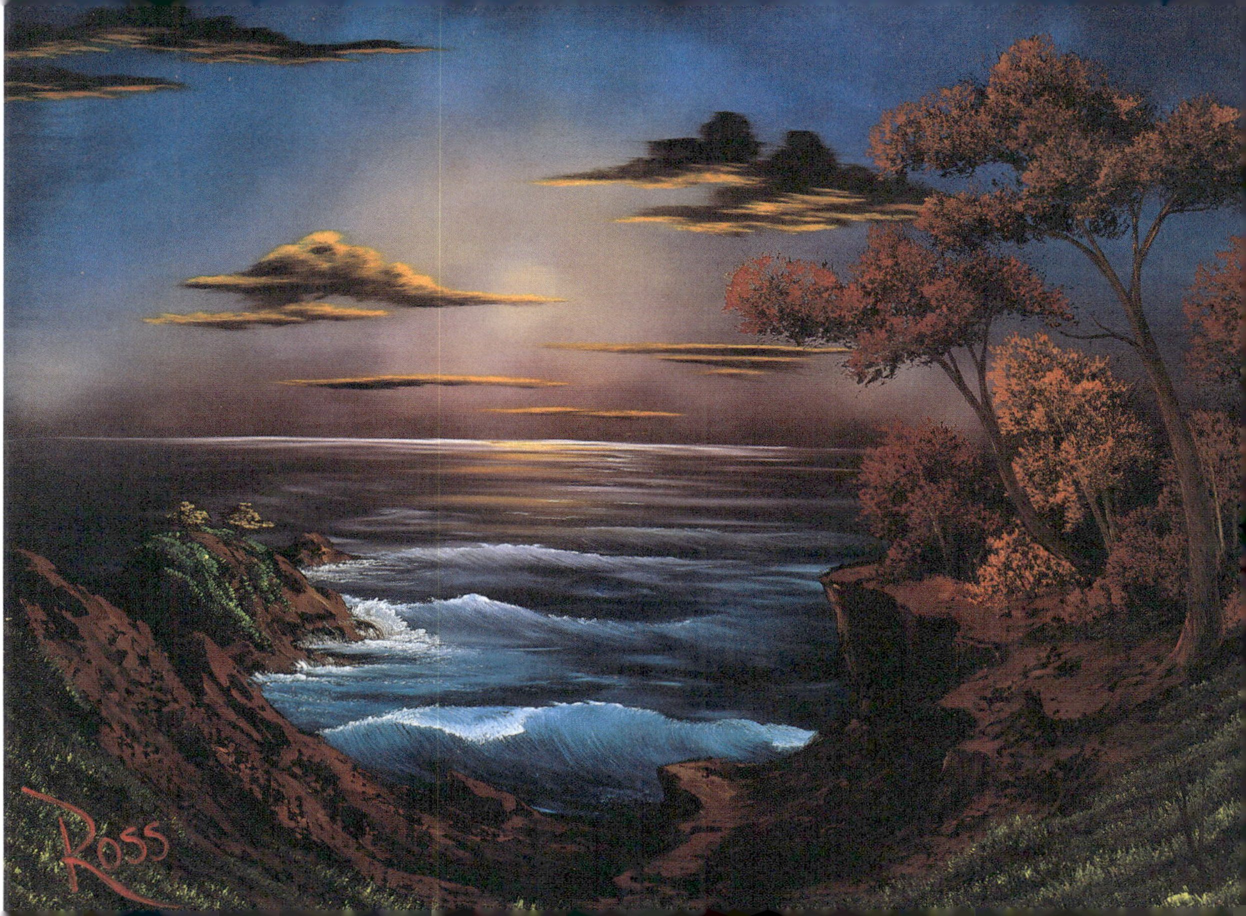
Ross

*Ebony Sea*
Season 2, Episode 3

**"We wish each and every one of you "Happy Painting."**

Bob Ross®

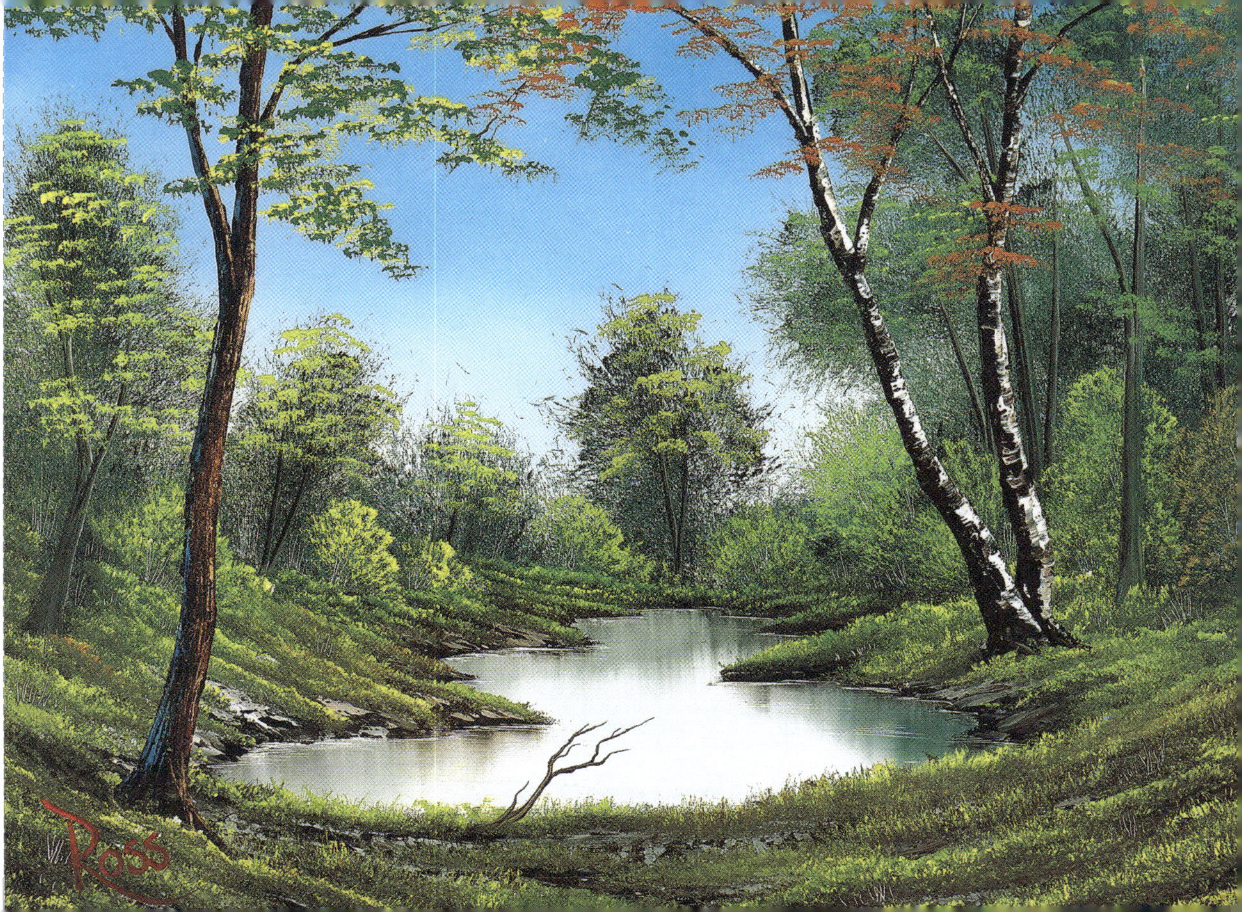
Ross

*Autumn Splendor*
Season 2, Episode 5

**"Let things happen. Create your own masterpiece."**

Bob Ross®



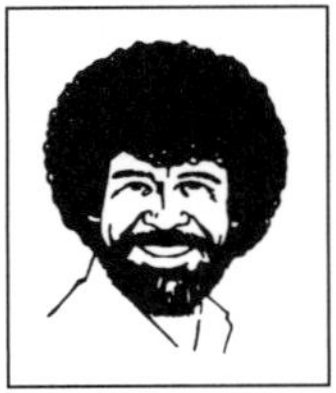

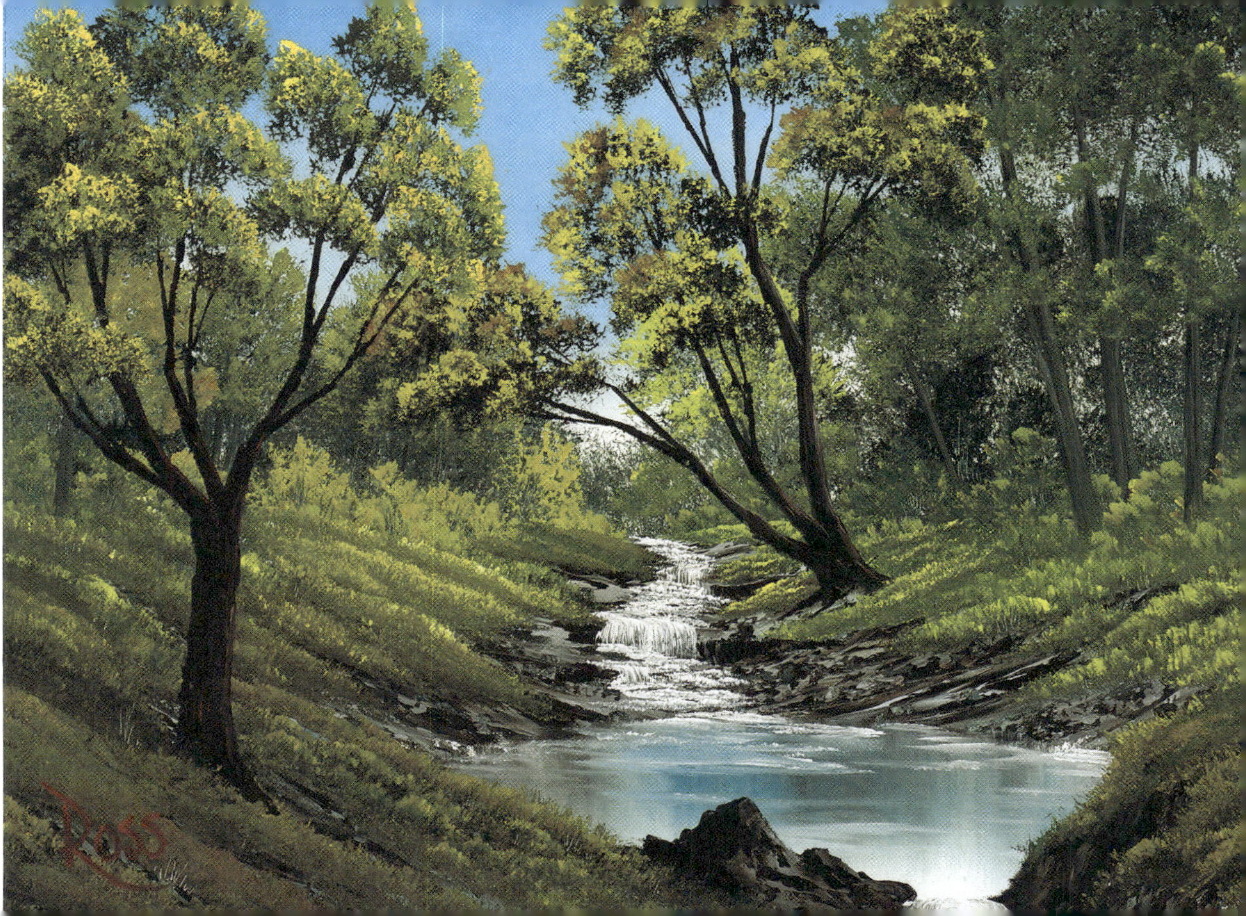

*Bubbling Stream*
Season 3, Episode 3

**"Don't spend a lot of time worrying about what you're going to paint. Just start painting."**

Bob Ross®

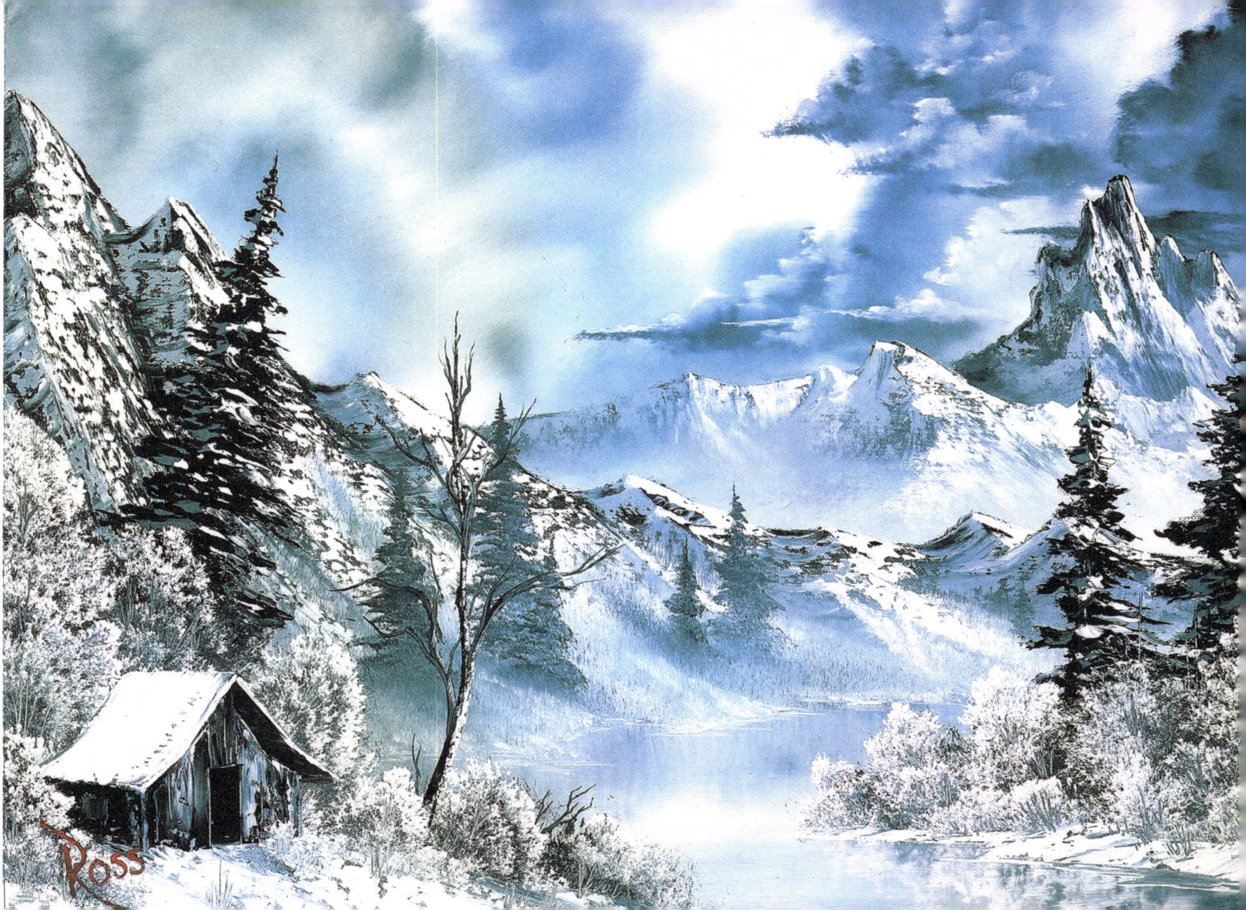
Ross

*Shades of Grey*
Season 2, Episode 4

**"All you need is a dream in your heart, and a happy little palette knife."**

Bob Ross®



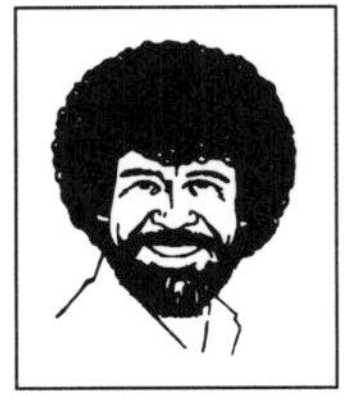

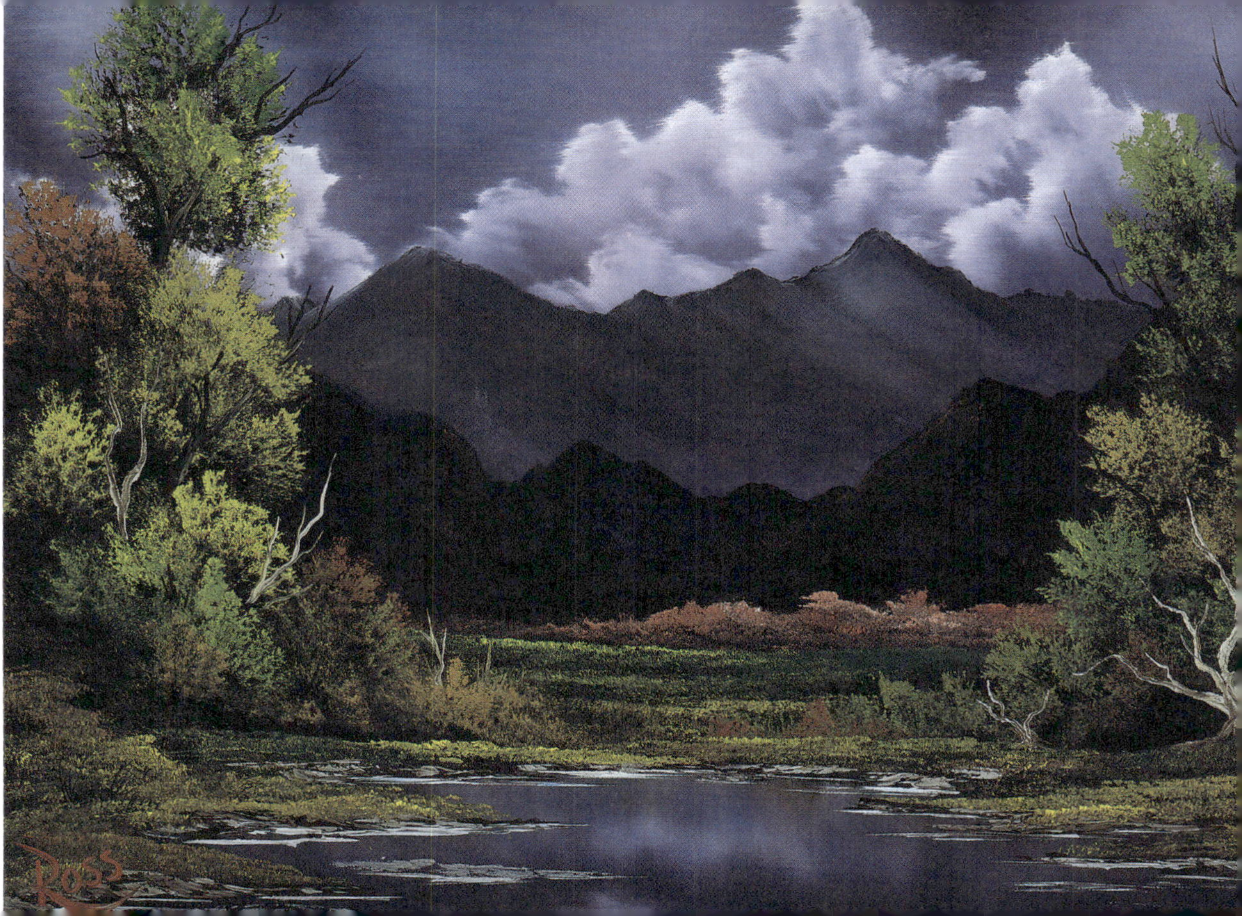
Ross

*Tranquil Valley*
Season 4, Episode 2

**"Little clouds are free. They float around and have fun, so just let them go wherever."**

Bob Ross®